YORK

Text by
ANGELA FIDDES

Photographs by
ERNEST FRANKL

PEVENSEY
Heritage Guides

York

Towering medieval walls encircle England's Eternal City, where almost 2000 years of history come alive in streets and squares, museums and ancient buildings, and in the great Minster of St Peter that stands sentinel over this magical place. York was settled by the Romans at the height of their empire in AD 71, as troops moved forward from Lincoln. It was conquered by the mighty Anglo-Saxon warlords in the 5th century and ruled over by Ivar the Boneless and his hordes of Danish Vikings in the 9th century. Beneath its streets, as well as above, York has a wondrous tale to tell, with a fascinating journey through Jorvik, the re-created Viking town from which the city took its name. The history of later periods is portrayed in an excellent wax museum, and in the Castle Museum where walks through Victorian and Edwardian streets and a glimpse into rooms furnished in styles from 1870 to 1953 provide a never-to-be-forgotten experience.

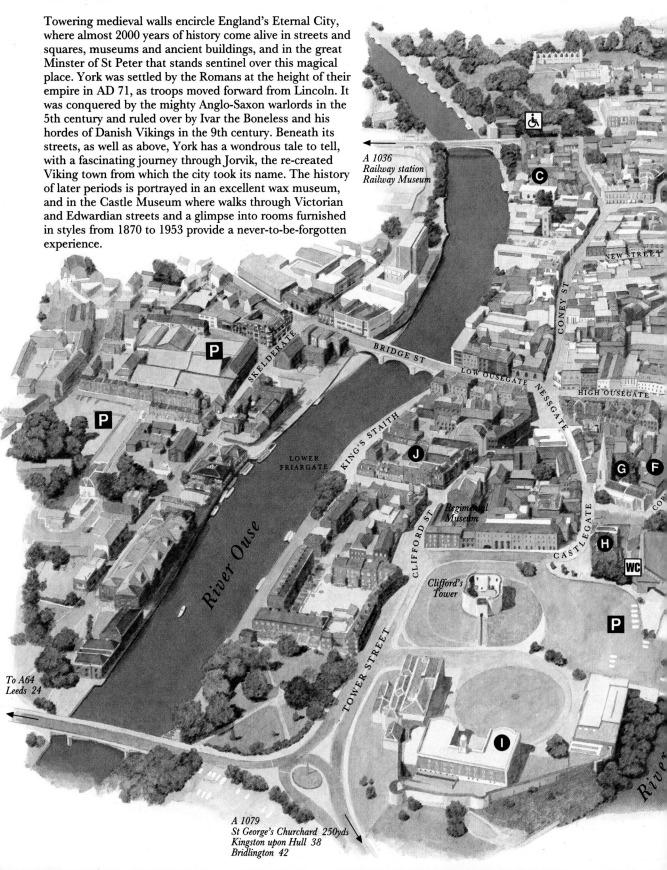

A 1036
Railway station
Railway Museum

NEW STREET

C

CONEY ST

P

SKELDERGATE

BRIDGE ST

LOW OUSEGATE

NESSGATE

HIGH OUSEGATE

P

LOWER FRIARGATE

KING'S STAITH

J

G

F

CLIFFORD ST

Regimental Museum

CASTLEGATE

H

WC

River Ouse

Clifford's Tower

P

TOWER STREET

To A64
Leeds 24

I

River

A 1079
St George's Churchard 250yds
Kingston upon Hull 38
Bridlington 42

PLACES TO SEE

Ⓐ Treasurer's House
National Trust. Apr-Oct, daily, Adm charge.
Tel (0904) 624247.

Ⓑ Shambles

Ⓒ The Guildhall
May-Oct, Mon-Sat and Sunday pm
Free entry. Tel (0904) 613161.

Ⓓ York Minster
Undercroft, Chapter House and Tower:
Mon-Sat and pm Sun. Adm charge.
Tel (0904) 624426.

Ⓔ Merchant Adventurers' Hall
Mid Mar-mid Nov, daily: mid Nov-mid Mar,
Mon-Sat. Adm charge. Tel (0904) 654818.

Ⓕ Jorvik Viking Centre
All year, daily. Adm charge.
Tel (0904) 643211

Ⓖ The York Story
All year, Mon-Sat and Sun pm.
Adm charge. Tel (0904) 628632.

Ⓗ Fairfax House
Mar-Dec, Mon-Thur, Sat, and Sun pm.
Adm charge. Tel (0904) 655543

Ⓘ Castle Museum
All year, daily. Adm charge.
Tel (0904) 653611.

Ⓙ Friargate Wax Museum
Daily, 10am-5pm; closed Dec and Jan.
Adm charge. Tel (0904) 658775.

YORK: THE HISTORIC CENTRE

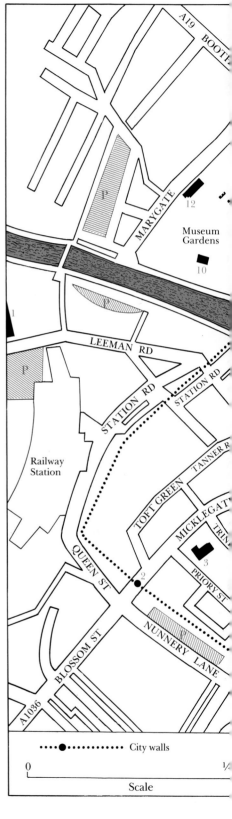

1	National Railway Museum	29	Minster Library
2	Micklegate Bar	30	Deanery
3	Holy Trinity Micklegate	31	Treasurer's House
4	Victoria Bar	32	St William's College
5	St Mary Bishophill Junior	33	Holy Trinity Goodramgate
6	St Martin cum Gregory	34	St Michael Spurriergate
7	York Arts Centre	35	All Saints Pavement
8	All Saints North Street	36	Jorvik Viking Centre
9	Lendal Tower	37	St Mary Castlegate (York Story)
10	Hospitium	38	Baile Hill
11	Yorkshire Museum	39	Assize Courts
12	St Olave Marygate	40	Castle Museum (Debtors' Prison)
13	St Mary's Abbey ruins	41	Castle Museum (Female Prison)
14	City Art Gallery	42	Clifford's Tower
15	King's Manor	43	Merchant Adventurers' Hall
16	Multangular Tower	44	Monk Bar
17	St Leonard's Hospital ruins	45	Merchant Taylors' Hall
18	City Library	46	St Cuthbert's
19	Tourist Information	47	St Anthony's Hall
20	Bootham Bar	48	Black Swan
21	Theatre Royal	49	Dorothy Wilson's Hospital
22	Assembly Rooms	50	St Denys Walmgate
23	Guildhall	51	Fishergate Postern Tower
24	Mansion House	52	Fishergate Bar
25	St Martin le Grand	53	Bowes Morrell House
26	St Helen Stonegate	54	Walmgate Bar
27	St Michael le Belfrey	55	Red Tower
28	York Minster	P	Parking

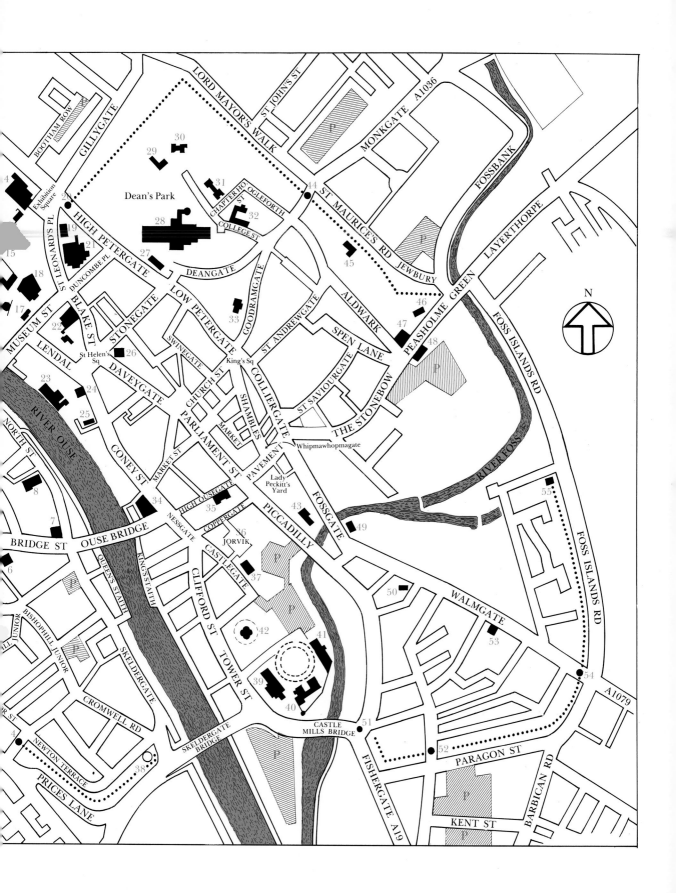

A Pevensey Heritage Guide

First published 1985
Reprinted 1990
Revised Edition 1993

Photographs: Ernest Frankl, except front cover: Skyscan Balloon Photography; 47: British Tourist
Authority

Permission to photograph within the Minster, granted by the Dean and Chapter, is gratefully
acknowledged

The assistance of Dr Richard Luckett is gratefully acknowledged

Colour map copyright © The Reader's Digest Association Ltd
All other maps by Carmen Frankl

A catalogue record for this book is available from the British Library.

ISBN 0 907115 70 5

Design by Book Production Consultants, Cambridge
Printed in Hong Kong by Wing King Tong Co. Ltd
for David & Charles plc
Brunel House Newton Abbot Devon

The Pevensey Press is an imprint of David & Charles plc

Front cover
Aerial view of York Minster from the east (*Skyscan Balloon Photography*)

Back cover
The beautiful wooden ceiling of the chapter house; the south façade of the Minster;
Bishopthorpe Palace, the home of the Archbishops of York

Title page inset
St Helen Stonegate, church of the Medieval glass painters: the window over the west door

Contents

History

The city of York is not instantly impressive to a visitor who approaches from afar; it is come upon suddenly, on low-lying land in the middle of the wide and flat Vale of York. But first appearances are deceptive, and York is rich in fine buildings reminding us of its prominent role in English history. Often acting as the unofficial capital of northern England, and on occasions as the national capital, it has for many centuries been an important centre of religion, administration, justice and trade. Its development from an early tribal settlement to the large and lively city of today encapsulates much of the history of England.

The first settlers on this spot chose it for several good reasons. Situated at the confluence of the Rivers Ouse and Foss, it was ideal for communication by water; the Ouse was navigable by sea-going vessels up to this point, and at the same time it was the first place, coming inland, where the river could be easily crossed, by ford and later by bridges. A ridge running east–west across the Vale of York, formed by a glacial moraine, provided a natural causeway over the wide and often marshy vale. This elevated land route across the 'neck of Britain' was probably an important thoroughfare from the Bronze Age onwards, linking Ireland with the mainland of Europe. Eminently defensible, the one major drawback of the site was the threat of flooding, a danger which still remains in the 20th century.

Eboracum, capital of Britannia Inferior

Geoffrey of Monmouth, the 12th-century historian, claimed for York a pre-Roman origin dating back to the time when David was king in Jerusalem. He stated that York was founded by a King Ebracus, who called the new settlement Kaerebrauc after himself. But there is little positive evidence as to who the earliest inhabitants of present-day York really were. The Romans called the fortress that they founded on the site Eboracum, which could mean either 'the place of the yews' or 'the estate of Eboros', the latter suggesting there was already some kind of settlement there. At the time of the Roman conquest of Britain the area was occupied by a powerful confederation of Celtic tribes, and one of their central strongholds was just a few miles upstream from the site of York, at Aldborough. Under their queen, Catimandua, the Brigantes formed a client kingdom of the Romans. Many of the tribesmen resented this dominion, and by AD 69 Catimandua had been replaced by her staunchly anti-Roman husband. This provoked the conquerors to assert their authority, and between 71 and 74 they brought the area under their control. A new fortress was needed to consolidate the gain and to

1 York's famous city walls in springtime, the mound covered with a mass of yellow daffodils. The walls were rebuilt in stone between 1250 and 1315, as the previous wooden defences began to prove an inadequate guard against increasingly sophisticated warfare techniques. Much of the money needed for their construction was raised by a tax (known as Murage) levied on all goods entering the city. Despite the strenuous efforts of the City Corporation in the 19th century to have them demolished, most of the walls survive today, and have been well restored; they extend for over two miles, and a walk along the footpaths on top is one of the best ways to see the city.

continue surveillance over the district, and the site of York was chosen for it.

The Romans' fortress was more or less the shape of a playing card (a rectangle with rounded edges) and occupied about 50 acres corresponding today roughly to the part of the city bounded by the Minster precincts. The natural advantages of the location were added to by building banks and timber walls around the perimeter, and new metalled roads linked it to existing routes. We know from a finely inscribed tablet dated 108 that the defences were reconstructed in stone at about that time, and the south-east gateway of the fortress was built. It appears that on at least two other occasions, around 200 and 300, the defences had to be rebuilt after attacks by warring tribes. These defences must have formed an impressive sight, with large interval towers punctuating the south-west flank, of which the Multangular Tower (**2**), built originally in the 4th century, is still standing.

The camp was laid out in the typical Roman manner, with a central headquarters building (where the Minster is now) and four gatehouses. Two main streets met near the centre: the Via Praetoria (approximately on the course of modern Stonegate), from the Praetorian Gate to the main fortress building, and the Via Principalis, crossing the camp from the north-west to the south-east gates. The IXth Legion, who had led the conquest of the area, were the original occupants of the fortress, but for some reason still unclear to modern scholars they disappeared without a trace between 108 and 122 – perhaps annihilated in battle, perhaps sent overseas in disgrace. The VIth Legion, who replaced them, stayed until at least the 4th century. The fortress was evidently a key stronghold, and was visited on occasions by the Emperor himself; in fact two Emperors died here, Septimus Severus (211) and Constantius Chlorus (306), and it was in York that Constantius' son, Constantine the Great, was first proclaimed Emperor (a fine head of him can be seen in the Yorkshire Museum, one of a splendid collection of artefacts from York's Roman period).

The fortress naturally attracted tradesmen, eager to sell their wares and offer their services to the soldiers, and soon a civilian settlement of *canabae* (booths) grew up to the north-west and along the quays of the Foss. Another and more important settlement developed to the south-east, across the Ouse. It was linked to the fortress at a point opposite the medieval Guildhall, and gradually took on the appearance of a town. Excavations have revealed a large bath building (in the Station Rise area), a large colonnaded basilica, fine tessellated pavements and hypocausts (in the Toft Green area) and numerous altars and dedication slabs to various gods. This settlement was granted the status of 'Colonia', the highest rank accorded to a chartered town, and became the capital of Britannia Inferior, a province which had been formed by the year 213 and encompassed most of Britain north of the River Trent. A surviving imperial decree, dated 5 May 210 and headed *Eboraci* (at York), shows that it was used by the imperial court during military campaigns against northern tribes. There was possibly some kind of palace here, for the Roman historian Suetonius refers to the Emperor Severus living in Eboracum in a *palatium*.

2 *Inside the Multangular Tower, an imposing survival of the Roman fortifications that once surrounded the city. The base, including the typical Roman red tile band, is 4th century, the upper part, with its thinner walls and arrow slits, being a late-13th-century rebuilding. Adjoining the tower, behind the Public Library, is a section of the original Roman wall, 150ft long and complete apart from the parapet on top.*

Saxon invasions and the first churches

Even before the withdrawal of the Roman troops at the beginning of the 5th century, York and the surrounding area seem to have been attacked by raiding parties from Scotland, Ireland and Germany. In 410 the Roman Emperor instructed English cities to defend themselves from such attacks. What actually happened in York, and in the rest of the country, is still far from clear, but excavations have suggested that some Roman buildings survived for several centuries thereafter, and they are likely to have been used by the native population. The defensive wall seems to have remained, and at one point, where presumably it had decayed, the so-called Anglian Tower was constructed.

The Anglo-Saxon invaders encountered vigorous local opposition during their gradual conquest of England. According to Welsh tradition (as related by Geoffrey of Monmouth), for much of the 5th century York remained in British hands, and was known as Cair Ebrauc. At one point it fell to the Saxons, but was recaptured by the legendary King Arthur. Legends apart, by the 6th century York lay within the Saxon kingdom of Deira which, with the neighbouring Bernicia, was to form Northumbria, one of the seven kingdoms into which England was divided during this period. For a time Northumbria was the most powerful kingdom of the Heptarchy, its kings being recognised as overlords by the rest of the country; but its supremacy was short lived, and by the 8th century it was a very minor state with an unclear line of succession – an easy target for invaders. In so far as such things existed at this time, York was the 'capital' of Northumbria; but judging from the Anglian place-names of the villages round York (such as Acomb, Heworth, Fulford, Langwith), the majority of the Anglian settlers preferred to live near the city rather than in it.

Christianity came to York during the latter part of the Roman occupation – the city sent a bishop to the Council of Arles in 314 – but it is likely that with the departure of the Romans, Christianity disappeared too. However, the memory of York's standing in Roman times must have lain behind Pope Gregory's plan, in the early 7th century, for the division of England into two metropolitan sees, one centred on London, the other on York. Although it was many years before this was put into effect, the foundation was laid by the conversion of King Edwin of Northumbria, after his marriage to a Christian Kentish princess. On Easter Day 627 he was baptised by her chaplain, Paulinus, in a hastily constructed wooden church. This church was dedicated to St Peter, and was thus the forerunner of the Minster. Its exact whereabouts are unknown, and though traditionally it was supposed to lie beneath the present Minster, recent excavations have revealed no trace of it.

Edwin did not long survive his conversion, being killed in battle in 632. Paulinus fled, but his work was continued by James the Deacon, and since 664 there has always been a Bishop of York (the see was elevated to the status of an Archbishopric in 735). The centres of northern Christianity remained the great monasteries, such as Jarrow and Hexham, until the accession of Egbert as Bishop in 732; he helped to found the School of York, which became renowned throughout Europe as one of the leading centres of international scholarship. The most famous master of the School, Alcuin, who eventually left York for the court of Charlemagne at Aachen, wrote a poem which contains the first surviving description of the city – 'built by the Romans, high with walls and towers'. The School possessed a magnificent library, which was tragically destroyed by fire in 1069.

The Anglo-Saxon town was known as Eferwic or Eoforwic – either a corruption of its Roman name, or derived from the Saxon word for 'boar' plus *wic*, market. Written references to a colony of Frisian merchants and finds of imported Rhineland pottery show that trade flourished with several parts of Europe. But archaeological evidence for this period is still relatively scarce, and little can be deduced about the size and layout of the town. It seems that a major change occurred about 800, when what remained of the Roman fortress was finally demolished. There was some

3 *The finest medieval font in York, in St Helen Stonegate. The bowl dates from the 12th century, the base is 13th century.*

development of the town to the north-west and the south; possibly twin towns grew up on either bank of the Ouse. An impressive architectural survival of this time, the tower of St Mary's Church in Bishophill Junior, is the oldest ecclesiastical building in York. The base is 10th century, made of re-used Roman materials, while the upper stages, though later, are pre-Conquest (note the herringbone work and typical Saxon windows). Inside, the tower arch is Saxon, and there are remains of a Saxon cross.

Jorvik, the Viking trade centre

In 866–7 York was captured by part of the great Danish army that had arrived in England the previous winter. During the next 80 years, with a few interruptions, it was the centre of a Scandinavian kingdom under Danish and Norse rule. This was a time of political instability and violence, some rulers surviving for only a few months, but it was also a time of considerable importance in the city's history. The newcomers called the town Jorvik, and it became a great river port on the Viking trade route, linked with Denmark, Norway, the Low Countries, and the Viking kingdom of Dublin. According to a monk writing in the late 10th century, Jorvik was a city 'crammed with merchandise . . . of traders who come from all parts, but especially Danes'. There was extensive development in the Pavement, Ousegate and Coppergate area, much of which was laid out as a market. Recent excavations here have greatly enhanced our knowledge of 'York town, the dank demesne', as it is evocatively called in a Viking saga. Among much else they have revealed that there was a wide variety of trades being carried on, indicating that Jorvik was a flourishing commercial centre. The modern visitor can have a taste of this world in its re-creation underneath the Coppergate precinct (see below, p. 61).

The Danes increased the walled area of the city, surrounding not only the old legionary fortress site, but also about 37 acres extending to the

4 The ancient street of Stonegate, in the heart of the city, contains architecture of almost every period in the last 800 years, beginning with these remains – fragmentary but of the greatest historical interest – of the oldest house in York in situ, a late-12th-century building behind No. 50 Stonegate. The two walls were discovered in 1939, when a later building in which they had been incorporated was being demolished, and they can now be viewed from what was the interior of the house.

Foss, where they had a harbour. On all sides but the south-east the Roman wall was covered by an earthen rampart topped with a timber palisade. The most prominent building must have been the royal palace – place-name evidence suggests it was near the present King's Square, possibly in the Roman south-east gatehouse. Many of York's street names still bear the ending 'gate', from the Old Norse *gata*, street.

Eric Bloodaxe, one of the most colourful and celebrated of the Danish kings, whose exploits are vividly described in the 13th-century Icelandic *Egil's Saga*, was expelled in 954. This really marked the end of a separate kingdom in the north with York as its capital. Control of the region now passed to the Earls, who resided in York, presumably in the area now known as Earlsborough. The most famous of the Earls was Siward, immortalised by Shakespeare in *Macbeth*, who was buried in the church of St Olave Marygate, which he had founded.

The northern capital of medieval England

The capture of York and the surrounding area proved to be one of the most difficult tasks facing William the Conqueror, for there was little readiness to accept the rule of an alien king in this part of the country. When rebellion broke out in 1068, William hurried north to exert his authority, and having quashed the uprising, he ordered the building of a castle in York. The following year there was a more serious revolt. Again William himself came north, defeated the rebels, pillaged the city, and had another castle built, on the opposite bank of the Ouse. Later that year the citizens supported a Danish raiding fleet, and succeeded in capturing the castles. This time William showed no mercy, and systematically ravaged the entire district between York and the River Tees. In the same year a great fire swept through the city. It was several years before York regained its former standing, and it did not rebel again.

The Domesday Book (1086) gives the first really clear picture of the city, containing details of population, religious foundations, and ownership of land – half of York was recorded as belonging to the king. One seventh of the city had been cleared for the building of the castles and the formation of the King's Pool. This vast moat, which submerged about 120 acres of arable land to the east, provided protection for the castle and supplied the castle and city ditches with water. The area remained waterlogged until the 19th century (it is now built on).

Gradually York managed to recover from the disasters of 1069. It continued to suffer from outbreaks of fire, a common hazard in medieval towns. The worst devastation happened in 1137, and few documents and even fewer buildings survive from before that date. But the Normans were prolific builders, rebuilding existing churches and constructing new ones: by the 13th century York had 40 parish churches, 34 within the city walls. They were also responsible for the foundation of the major religious houses, St Mary's Abbey, St Leonard's Hospital and Holy Trinity Priory, as well as a host of lesser ones. The Minster was rebuilt on a vast scale by Archbishop Thomas of Bayeux from 1080 onward (later rebuildings have erased most of his work). Building of the city walls on top of the massive Danish earth bank began in the mid 13th century; they

enclosed about 263 acres. In the Micklegate and central areas they were probably completed around 1270, while the Walmgate section seems to have been built after 1345. Long stretches of the walls still encircle the city, and walking along them is one of the quintessential pleasures of visiting York. From the first they were pierced by four major gates known as bars, each entrance being blocked by an inner gate and outer gate with portcullis in front. The walls, together with the castle, King's Pool and the two rivers, completely surrounded the city in a defensive ring.

One of the ugliest incidents in the city's history occurred in 1190. Like several other English cities, York had a fair-sized Jewish community in the Norman period. Anti-Jewish sentiment was stirred up after an incident at Richard I's coronation, and some of those who were in debt to the Jews in York took advantage of it to launch an attack on the community, many of whom took refuge in the castle. There they soon found themselves under siege, and many committed suicide at the bidding of one of their religious leaders, while others who surrendered on the promise of safety were cruelly massacred. All records of debts owed to the Jews were burned in the Minster, where they had been stored. Some of the community must have survived, for the city's Jewish population reached its peak in the early 13th century, when it included among its members Aaron of York, the wealthiest Jewish financier of the 13th century. Many of the richest Jews, including Aaron, lived in Coney Street, whilst others lived in adjacent Market Street, known until recently as Jubbergate.

York played a signal role in national affairs in the early Middle Ages, for it was a major administrative centre – the capital of the northern province of the Church and headquarters of the king's sheriff, as well as a substantial trading and market centre. Its stature increased when war with Scotland made it necessary to move the offices of the government of England to York in 1298. They remained there for seven years, and returned on later occasions. The presence of the Courts of the Exchequer and Chancery, the royal law courts and councils of all sorts proved a great stimulus to York's economy, as did its new role as the centre of a war administration. There was fighting and raiding in the whole area between York and the Highlands of Scotland. On one occasion in 1319, part of the Scottish army almost reached the city walls before the Archbishop and Mayor could raise a defending army; they managed to stave off the immediate threat, but were then disastrously defeated at Myton on Swale (about 15 miles from York), where many citizens, including the Mayor, were killed. After 1337 danger from France assumed greater importance, and though the Scottish threat remained, it was increasingly regarded as a regional problem. York briefly became the centre of government again in 1392, when Richard II, having quarrelled with the people of London, transferred the offices of state for a few months. Although he abandoned plans for creating York his permanent capital, the city retained a special place in his affections, and in charters of 1393 and 1396 he granted it special privileges which made it a corporate borough and county of itself. This formed the final part of the structure of self-government which the city had gained throughout the preceding centuries, and which remained basically unchanged until the 19th century.

5 *This graceful late Norman arcade – it may have been part of a cloister – is all that remains, apart from the chapel (which has been restored), of the former Archbishop's Palace in the Minster precincts. The Archbishop of York's residence is now at Bishopthorpe (see overleaf).*

6 *Bishopthorpe Palace, the home of the Archbishops of York, lies a few miles from the city centre. Begun in the mid 13th century by Archbishop Walter de Grey, it now presents a chiefly 18th-century 'Gothick' appearance, thanks to the work of Thomas Atkinson, who was commissioned by Archbishop Drummond in the 1760s to bring a sense of order to the rather disparate group of buildings. Details that have lasted from other eras of its long history include 13th-century lancet windows and a fine 15th-century chimney. The palace is not open to the public, but is used by many people connected with the Church and its community.*

Medieval York became the second largest provincial city of the realm, and one of the very wealthiest. Its prosperity was reflected in splendid new buildings, notably the parish churches, with their fine stained glass, and the guildhalls. Not all was splendour, however. There was much squalor in this densely populated city, where those living within the walls numbered approximately four times present-day figures. In 1332 Edward III wrote to the Mayor and bailiffs, complaining that the smell and filth of the streets of York were the worst in the kingdom. The commercial prosperity was largely based on the wool trade, and later the cloth trade, but there were numerous other crafts in the city too, each closely controlled by its own guild company. York was especially renowned for its glass painters, some of whose work can still be seen today. Wealthy merchants provided the necessary patronage, while the raw material (until the 16th century most glass was imported) could come up-river from the port of Hull.

The guilds were responsible for what must have been one of the most spectacular pieces of pageantry each year, the performance of the Mystery Plays during the Feast of Corpus Christi. The cycle of 48 plays tells the Biblical story from the Creation to the Last Judgement. Each play was put on by a different guild, some guilds having links with the topic of their play. For example, the Shipwrights performed the building of the Ark, the Fishermen and Mariners the story of the Flood, the Vintners the Wedding at Cana. The plays were enacted on wagons known as 'pageants', which processed through the city, stopping for performances at about 12 set points. The procession started outside Holy Trinity Priory in Micklegate at about 4.30 in the morning and finished at dusk in Pavement. High standards were expected, and fines were levied on those who did not know their parts, or played them in a casual manner. After the Reformation, feeling grew that the plays were superstitious and unsuitable, and in 1572 all copies of them were called in for correction, and never returned. Fortunately one copy, now in the British Library, survived; and nowadays the Mystery Plays are performed at three- or four-yearly intervals in the dramatic setting of the ruins of St Mary's Abbey (**22**).

Reformation and rebellion

During the late 15th century York's prosperity began to decline, largely because of a depression in the local textile trade. Powerful and ever-increasing competition came from the Hanseatic League, from London merchants, and from spinning and weaving communities around the new textile towns of the West Riding. Moreover, the new ships now being built were too large to sail up the Ouse as far as York, so the city lost its importance as a port and became more and more of a regional market. Its fortunes seem to have been at their lowest ebb between 1510 and 1560; by the 1520s its rank among provincial towns had fallen to fifteenth. There were outbreaks of bubonic plague throughout the 16th century and the population dropped sharply, possibly by as much as one third. It seems that very few houses were built or rebuilt during these years, a sure sign of a town in decay.

7 *A popular way of seeing the major sights of York – a ride in a pony and trap, here seen about to set off from just outside the Minster in High Petergate.*

8 *Georgian York was the social capital of the north of England, and the city is full of excellent 18th-century domestic architecture. These four doorways are a sample of the innumerable rewarding details that enliven a short walk through the centre: (top left) Garforth House, Nos. 52–4 Micklegate, completed by 1757; (top right) the Diocesan Board of Finance in College Street, early Georgian; (bottom left) Peasholme House, St Saviour's Place, 1752; (bottom right) Micklegate House, Nos. 88–90 Micklegate, 1753.*

The Reformation also had far-reaching economic effects in York. The dissolution of the monasteries meant an enormous loss of patronage, and thus employment, in the city, which had depended heavily on the business brought to its tradesmen by clergy, monks and pilgrims within its walls and the northern monasteries beyond them. Many monastic buildings were destroyed, and some of York's finest architecture was lost. The suppression of the smaller monasteries in 1536 was the immediate cause of the northern rebellion known to history as the Pilgrimage of Grace, although its inspiration was not purely religious – its leaders, who marched under the banner of the Five Wounds of Christ, also harboured economic grievances. Their belief that the government neglected the north for the sake of the south was reflected in their demand that no man dwelling north of the Trent should be expected to appear at any King's Court other than at York. Led by Robert Aske, the rebels marched peaceably into York, and during the short time they occupied the city some of the monks were repossessed. Eventually they were tricked into surrendering, the leaders were condemned to death, and Aske was hung alive in chains from Clifford's Tower.

However, the aftermath of the Pilgrimage of Grace benefited York, for in 1537 the government reconstituted the King's Council – a powerful judicial and administrative body, originally set up during the reign of Richard III to control the north on behalf of the Privy Council. This was important for the future development of the city, for it made York once again the capital of northern England, and a key centre of justice. As the permanent place of residence of a great household it attracted an increasing volume of trade, and many came to seek justice in the courts. The period of decline was halted, and prosperity gradually returned.

In the 17th century York briefly resumed prominence in national affairs. In 1639 Charles I made it the centre of English military preparations in the Bishops' War against Scotland. Then in March 1642, during the early part of the Civil War between King and Parliament, Charles, incensed at the behaviour of the population of London towards him, moved the royal court to York, and the city remained the royal capital of England until August of that year, and the royalist northern military centre until 1644. This was the year of the protracted siege of York, from April to June, by Parliamentary forces; the significance attached by both sides to the siege testifies to the city's importance as a northern capital as well as a military stronghold. 'If York be lost I shall esteem my crown little else', declared Charles. York was eventually lost, for although Prince Rupert succeeded in raising the siege, the following day the royalist forces were disastrously defeated at the Battle of Marston Moor (7 miles west of York). York now became a Parliamentary garrison, but was never again involved in hostilities. Thanks to the intervention of the Parliamentary commander Lord Fairfax, a local landowner (and patron of the poet Marvell), many of York's ecclesiastical treasures, especially the painted glass, escaped the destruction inflicted by the Parliamentarians in so many other towns. The terms of York's surrender clearly stipulated that 'neither church nor any building shall be defaced', and Fairfax ensured that they were strictly observed.

The city was to face the possibility of attack by an army on one more occasion. After the successes of the Jacobite rebels in Scotland in 1745, and their subsequent march south, York was put into a state of defence. But fears for its safety proved groundless. Following the Jacobites' sweeping defeat at the Battle of Culloden, 22 of the rebels were brought to York to be executed. The heads of some of them were displayed on Micklegate Bar, and only removed several years later – the last time this barbaric practice was used.

Society, industry and the modern age

As we can tell from the wealth of surviving Georgian architecture, both private houses and public buildings, York was transformed in the 18th century into a social centre of consequence for the northern gentry, many of whom had their town residences in the city. A large part of the population was engaged in producing luxury goods and providing services for the monied classes; 'Here is no trade indeed, except such as depends upon the confluence of the gentry', commented Daniel Defoe in his *Tour through Great Britain* (1724). Various attractions were provided for the amusement of visitors, including regular race meetings. These were always popular and were held on Knavesmire, an open tract of land to the south of the city, where a new grandstand was erected (1753) to the designs of the local architect John Carr. Carr (1723–1808) was one of the most successful provincial architects of the 18th century, and examples of his work can be seen throughout the city and the surrounding countryside. Assemblies, primarily a winter event, were also held during race week; the magnificent Assembly Rooms (**47**), designed by Lord Burlington, were opened in 1732. The first theatre on the site of the present Theatre Royal was built in 1714.

Lying on the main route between London and Scotland, York was a great coaching centre in the 18th century, full of inns. Among the best known were the George and the Black Swan in Coney Street (both now demolished). The busy coach traffic brought some attendant hazards, such as the danger of highwaymen: John Revison and Dick Turpin were both noted in and around York. The latter was famous for such exploits as riding from London to York on his horse Black Bess in 15 hours – an impossible feat, but perpetuated in romantic fiction, for example Harrison Ainsworth's *Rookwood* (1834). Justice eventually caught up with Turpin, and he was hung on Knavesmire in 1739, his body being buried in St George's churchyard. More law-abiding residents of 18th-century York included Francis Drake, whose *Eboracum* (1736) provides the first comprehensive and accurate history of the city, and the novelist Laurence Sterne, whose most famous work, *Tristram Shandy*, was first published in the city – Sterne drew widely on local persons and events as butts for his satire.

There had been a small but steadily increasing Quaker element in York ever since George Fox's visit in 1671; the first meeting house was built in Friargate in 1674. The Quakers endowed the city by founding the Retreat (1796), an institution for the care of the mentally ill which was widely known for its humane methods of treatment; the Mount, a girls' school opened in 1784; and a boys' school that later became Bootham

9 *York provides many enjoyable instances of early and later styles combined in a single building (see also, for example, St William's College, **52**). No. 10 Stonegate, a half-timbered structure with an overhanging upper storey, is probably basically medieval, but in Victorian times it was given a new frontage and covered with brightly coloured Minton tiles.*

School (1829). They also played a signal role in the city's economic life, for the confectionery business which York has long been known for was started in the 18th century by two Quaker families. The Tuke family manufactured cocoa and chocolate behind their shop in Castlegate, beginning the business that was transferred to Henry Rowntree in 1862, while the firm of Terry and Sons was established in St Helen's Square in 1767 under the name of Blaydon and Berry.

The confectionery industry grew steadily during the 19th century, but the industrial revolution that transformed so many of the towns of the north of England into great manufacturing centres made very little impact on York. It continued to be a city of small craftsmen, run on traditional lines. Some local businesses did attract national renown, such as the iron foundry firm of Walkers, who were appointed ironfounders to Queen Victoria in 1847, and supplied the gates and railings for the newly constructed British Museum in 1850. Much was changed by the arrival of the railway in 1839 (the first train from York to London ran in 1840). Once again York was important as a route centre, being now a terminus for north- and south-bound traffic between London and Scotland. Ancillary railway services created employment and stimulated local industry. Much of the impetus in bringing the railway to York was given by George Hudson, the 'railway king'. On the basis of his chairmanship of a group of amalgamated railway companies he became the most influential man in York, and was several times Lord Mayor. Determined to see York established as the heart of the railway network, he seems to have been rather over-zealous in his efforts, for in 1849 various financial frauds in which he had been involved came to light, and his downfall was immediate and total. His enemies resolved to obliterate any memory of his name and work, and Hudson Street was renamed Railway Street (it reverted to its

10 *York University, founded in 1962, lies two miles south-east of the city at Heslington. The architects were Robert Matthew, Johnson-Marshall and Partners. One of the most striking buildings is the Central Hall (1968), a half-octagon which looks almost top-heavy under its aluminium roof. The canted sides face the lake, the upper storeys being cantilevered.*

11 *When it was first built, in 1877, York station was held to be the largest in Europe. Thomas Prosser designed this magnificent curved train shed, 800ft long, its roof supported by slender Corinthian columns. The platforms were extended in 1900 and 1909, and extra platforms were added in 1938. York is still a major centre of Britain's railway network, and is now the home of the National Railway Museum (see 32).*

original name only in 1970, on the hundredth anniversary of his death). Today the railway is still important in the life of the city, though it has been superseded as the largest employer by the confectionery business.

York received a new addition in 1962 with the opening of the University (**10**), just outside the city, centred round the 16th-century Heslington Hall. It has proved popular with students from all parts of the country and from overseas, and its architecture, by Robert Matthew, Johnson-Marshall and Partners, under the direction of Andrew Derbyshire, has been praised as being amongst the most successful of all the new universities.

Modern York has many attractions. It is one of the few remaining walled cities in Britain, despite the efforts of the City Corporation in the early 19th century to remove the walls and bars (fortunately they encountered a vigorous and concerted protest, led by such notables as the artist Sir William Etty and the novelist Sir Walter Scott). Today the entire historic core of the city is protected, as it has been designated a conservation area. The major restoration of the Minster, the opening of the National Railway Museum and the Jorvik Viking Centre, and the additions to the Theatre Royal have all increased the pleasure the city offers the visitor. But York is more than a historic showpiece. As the seat of an Archbishop it is the centre of Church administration in northern England. As an Assize town it is a judicial centre. It provides a vital link in the modern railway network. It has a thriving University. All in all, York is a happy marriage of past and present.

The Minster

Historical background

The first church to be built on or near the site of the Minster was the wooden structure in which King Edwin was baptised in 627. Soon afterwards, the king ordered the building of a stone church to replace it, but he was killed in battle before its completion, and the work was finished under his successor, Oswald. The exact whereabouts of this building remain a mystery: excavations in the late 1960s revealed no trace (though they did unearth remains of the headquarters of the Roman legionary fortress). By the time St Wilfrid came to York as Bishop in 669 the church was in considerable disrepair, and he set about putting it in order, having the roof covered with lead and the windows glazed. The Minster seems to have been burnt down in 741 and subsequently rebuilt, but very little is known about this new building either.

The building was already in a state of decay when the fire which swept through the city in 1069 damaged it severely. A year later Thomas of Bayeux was appointed Archbishop by William the Conqueror and almost at once began rebuilding. Work was probably finished by the time of his death in 1100. The new cathedral was on a true east–west alignment, aslant the now almost flattened remains of the Roman headquarters building, and caused major changes in the city's street pattern. It had a long apsed chancel and a great aisleless nave; by the standards of the time it was an enormous building, about 361 ft (110 m) long and 45 ft (14 m) wide. The extent of the apse can be traced in the undercroft. The position and scale of the central crossing of the present Minster, as well as the great width of its nave and the overall breadth of the west front, were all determined by this building. The fire of 1137 caused damage to an unknown extent, and necessitated some rebuilding. The first major change came in 1154, under Archbishop Roger Pont l'Evêque, with the construction of a magnificent choir, raised high upon a crypt (part of which can be seen in the undercroft). Then in about 1220 Archbishop Walter de Grey initiated work on a new south transept, and for the next 250 years construction of the building was carried on almost continually. The nave was begun in 1291 and a new choir about 70 years later.

It was not until 1472 that the Dean and Chapter decided that rebuilding was complete, and on 3 July of that year a great rededication service was held to mark the occasion. After this there were few structural alterations to the Minster. The Reformation caused the removal of the shrine of St William (see below, p. 41) and various other fittings considered popish,

12 *The nave of York Minster, looking west. The nave altar is in the foreground. The black and white marble floor was designed by Lord Burlington, the great 18th-century patron of the arts, who had extensive estates in Yorkshire; it was laid between 1730 and 1736. The wooden vault replaces the original, which perished in the fire of 1840.*

together with the destruction of chantry chapels. In 1730 Lord Burlington designed a new floor, of black and white marble in a key-pattern design. It took six years to lay, and is still in place (**12**). Cleaning of the interior in the late 18th century unfortunately included the obliteration of surviving medieval gilding and painting underneath thick lime and ochre wash.

Two tragic incidents in the 19th century caused incalculable destruction. The first was in 1829, when a religious lunatic, Jonathan Martin, hid himself in the Minster after Evensong and set light to the choir. The fire was not discovered until the following morning, and not extinguished until that evening. By then all the woodwork of the choir, its 14th-century roof and some of the medieval stained glass had been destroyed; the organ and a valuable collection of music manuscripts also perished. The excellent restoration work was supervised by Sir Robert Smirke. In 1840 an almost equally disastrous fire broke out, this time accidentally, in the south-west tower. It spread quickly to the nave roof, which collapsed, thus preventing the entire building from being engulfed. None the less, the south-west tower was gutted, the nave piers were badly cracked, and the west doors were largely destroyed. Restoration was directed by Sidney Smirke, but public response to the appeal for finance was far less forthcoming than on the previous occasion.

Major restoration work has also been carried out in this century. A survey of the fabric by the architect Bernard Feilden in 1967 revealed a structural crisis of terrifying proportions. The Minster was found to be in very real danger of collapse, and within 15 years would be unable to withstand the repairs necessary to save it. An appeal was launched in May that year for £2 million to finance the work, and money poured in from all parts of the world. Colossal new foundations were laid at the east and west ends of the building; the piers of the central towers were strengthened with collars of concrete attached to the Norman foundations by 20,000 ft (6100 m) of steel rods, and the central tower itself was braced by steel girdles and reroofed. The interior stonework was also repaired. In 1972 the 500th anniversary of the completion of the fabric was celebrated, and, at the same time, the successful completion of this major rescue operation. It seemed that the Minster was at last secure, but in the early hours of 9 July 1984 disaster struck again. A fire, apparently started by lightning, destroyed the roof of the south transept, and was only narrowly prevented from spreading into the crossing and nave. Stonework and the famous rose window were badly damaged. Repair work began immediately, continuing a process of rebuilding and restoration that has had few pauses during the Minster's 13 centuries.

A tour of the Minster

The exterior This is England's largest medieval church, but despite its immense size the Minster does not visually dominate its city in the way that the cathedrals of Durham or Lincoln, for instance, command theirs. This is largely because it is built on the level; to get a good view from a distance the spectator needs to be some way above the ground. The effect is impressive even from the relatively modest height of the city walls. Close to, however, as the building rears up at the end of the narrow

central streets, or seen from Dean's Park, its scale is overwhelming. Internally it is 486 ft (148 m) long and the central tower is 198 ft (60 m) high. The plan is quite simple; a long nave, transepts, and an even longer choir and presbytery, with choir transepts. On the north side the view is interrupted by the late-13th-century octagonal chapter house, the largest in England, which has massive buttresses. On the south side the main transept is flanked by some low buildings, including the 14th-century Zouche Chapel on the far right and the former Library, now the Bookshop and Choir Practice Room, on the left. The west front rises up to two towers, the last part of the Minster to be built; the southern one dates from *c*1430-50, the northern from *c*1470, two years before the Minster was finally consecrated. The most memorable feature of this imposing façade is the huge central window, completed in 1338, whose flowing tracery describes a heart shape (**14**).

Nave (12) The foundation stone of the present nave was laid in 1291, but nearly 70 years passed before it was completed, and changes in style had to be assimilated along the way. Although this is the widest medieval nave in England, its slender piers greatly increase the vertical emphasis, as do the pronounced vaulting shafts, which run unbroken from the floor to the springing of the vault. This effect was increased even more by the incorporation of triforium and clerestory into one large window (probably the first time in England that they were treated as one). All the high

vaults of the Minster are wooden – their span was too great for stone vaulting to have been possible. That of the nave is a copy of the original which was destroyed in the fire of 1840. Along its apex can be seen eight main bosses depicting scenes from the New Testament. A figure of St Peter, to whom the Minster is dedicated, stands between the two central west doors. Above is the huge expanse of 14th-century glass in the great west window (the faces of the botton row of figures date from the 18th century). High on the nave walls, shields proclaim the heroism of northern families who fought with Edward II against the Scots, and who contributed to the building of the nave. The walls of the aisles have lavishly carved blank arcading. The glass of the aisle windows is a unified scheme, installed c1310–20; bands of grisaille (uncoloured) glass alternate with scenes in coloured glass, forming the impression of long strips of colour stretching from end to end of the aisles – an important horizontal accent in a building where the emphasis is so much on the verticals.

Crossing and transepts Above ground, the earliest visible parts of the Minster are the transepts, the south (c1220–40) being slightly earlier than the north (c1240–60). Both are in the Early English style, with piers of clustered shafts and Purbeck marble columns, and both are full of rich detail, especially the north, where figures of animals appear among the fine stiff-leaf carving. In the north wall of the north transept are five magnificent lancets containing grisaille glass of c1250 and known collectively as the Five Sisters Window. Charles Dickens, who was fascinated by this window, recounted a purely fictional tale of five sisters who worked lengths of tapestry and then had them copied in glass as a memorial to the youngest, who had died. The window was restored in the 1920s in memory of women of the Empire who died in World War I; it was releaded with lead from Rievaulx Abbey which had lain buried in the grounds of the abbey since its dissolution.

The rose window in the south transept contains early-16th-century glass and commemorates the marriage of Henry VII and Elizabeth of York (1486), which brought to an end the Wars of the Roses. The sunflower in the centre was painted by William Peckitt in the 18th century. In the south transept is the superb 13th-century tomb of Walter de Grey: his Purbeck marble effigy lies on a low chest with a high canopy. When the coffin lid was removed during restoration in 1968, it was found to be decorated with a life-size painting of the Archbishop. Also found in the tomb were a ring with a large uncut sapphire, and the Archbishop's chalice, paten and pectoral staff (these are now all on view in the undercroft museum).

The crossing is directly under the central tower, which was rebuilt in the 15th century to replace one that had collapsed. Henry IV sent his master mason, William of Colchester, to supervise the work. William's original plan of a belfry above the lantern stage was somewhat modified, presumably because of the inadequacy of the foundations (the Minster bells hang in the west towers). From the crossing it is possible to look up at the central tower's distant ceiling, which is the original one. The huge boss in the middle, 4 ft 9 in (1.5 m) in diameter, shows St Peter with the gospels and a sword.

The entrance to the choir is flanked by a splendid asymmetrical screen (**15**), built *c*1475–1506, whose niches contain representations of all the kings of England from William the Conqueror to Henry VI (reading left to right). They are all the original sculptures except for the figure of Henry VI, which was removed out of fear that it might become a shrine to the murdered monarch (a replacement was provided in 1810). The screen is often attributed to William Hyndeley, master mason, but it is probably earlier – possibly a design by William of Colchester, built after his death.

Choir and eastern arm The scale of the nave was maintained in the rebuilding of the eastern arm of the Minster. The Zouche Chapel (**16**; it takes its name from an Archbishop of York) was begun in 1350, when the Norman choir still stood, in a style quite distinct from any other surviving part of the building; it has a fine vault, supported on Purbeck marble shafts. The rest of the east end consists of the choir, one-bay choir transepts and the four-bay Lady Chapel. It follows the style of the nave fairly closely, with adjustments in the details. The Lady Chapel was built first (1361–70). In its great east window is the world's largest surviving expanse of medieval glass in a single window. This was the work of John Thornton of Coventry, a master glass painter, who received 4 shillings a week for his labours, with an additional £5 a year, and £10 on completion of the task, which took him – with the help of several assistants – three years (1405–8). The glass tells the story of God as Alpha and Omega. He appears in the central light at the very top, while those who praise Him

15 *The choir screen, designed in the 1470s and finished in the early 16th century, incorporates statues of all the kings of England from William I to Henry VI. The sculptor may have been William Hyndeley, recorded as the mason responsible for building the screen.*

16 *The Zouche Chapel, looking east. This chapel was added to the Minster in the mid 14th century to commemorate Archbishop Zouche. The 15th-century muniment cupboards built into its north wall were used for centuries to store the Minster's treasures.*

32

17 *The beautiful wooden ceiling of the chapter house is unsupported by any central pillar, which creates a memorable effect of spaciousness. The present ceiling, painted by Thomas Willement in 1844–5 and since restored, is a replacement of the original oak panelling, which is thought to have collapsed (because of woodworm) in the late 18th century.*

(angels, patriarchs, prophets and saints) are depicted in the tracery. Narrative panels in the main lights illustrate the words alpha and omega, the first three rows containing 27 scenes from the Old Testament, from the Creation to the death of Absalom, and the next nine containing 81 scenes from the Revelation of St John. The bottom row shows legendary and historical figures associated with early Christianity in northern England. Kneeling before an altar in the centre light is Walter Skirlaw, Bishop of Durham, who financed the glazing of the window; he probably hoped that this gift would improve his chance of obtaining the see of York, but he was unsuccessful.

All the woodwork and the ceiling of the choir were destroyed in the fire of 1829; their replacements are copies of the originals. At the west end of the north choir aisle is the only royal tomb in the Minster, that of Prince William of Hatfield, son of Edward III, who died in 1346 at the age of eight, whilst staying at nearby Doncaster. His father had married Philippa of Hainault in the Minster in 1328, a spectacular event attended by almost all the nobility of England. Most of the Minster's good post-medieval monuments are in the north and south choir aisles.

18 *One of the seven windows of the chapter house. Originally glazed in 1300–7, they show a new approach to window design, with figure panels set between bands of grisaille to allow for extended narrative sequences. The panels depict episodes from the life of Christ and from the lives of Sts Catherine, Thomas à Becket, Peter, Paul, Denis, Margaret, Nicholas, John the Baptist and Edmund.*

Chapter house and vestibule The chapter house was built *c*1260–85. Here the business of the Minster is conducted and synods and convocations met, for this is not consecrated ground. It is remarkable for the fact that despite its size, no central pillar supports the roof, which is leaded without and timbered within, one of the finest medieval roofs in England (**17**). It seems that a stone ceiling was planned but proved technically impossible. The present ceiling, of oak bosses and lath and plaster infill, replaces the original oak panelling, which is believed to have collapsed because of the effects of woodworm sometime before 1798, the date of the replacement. The chapter house is an outstanding example of the Decorated period of architecture: the magnificent stalls around the edge of the room have the lush stiff-leaf and naturalistic carving and lavish use of Purbeck marble shafts characteristic of the style. There are representations in stone (originally painted) of all sorts of plants, including hawthorn, vine, hop and maple. The projecting canopies of the stalls, carved into pendants at the front, give an undulating rhythm to the wall. Above the entrance doorway are niches said formerly to have contained silver statues of Christ and the Apostles, and next to the door (to the left as one enters) are the words 'ut rosa flos florum sic est domus ista domorum' (as the rose is the flower of flowers, so is this the room of rooms). Much of the glass (**18**) belongs to the original glazing scheme of *c*1285; it is the earliest series of narrative panels in the Minster to survive *in situ*, though severe corrosion has meant considerable replacement over the years. The figure panels alternate with strips of grisaille glass to form bands of colour across the lights.

The vestibule is the passage that leads from the north transept to the chapter house; it has rich blank arcading and very splendid tracery. The original chapter house doors have superb late-13th-century swirling ironwork, incorporating, at the top, attenuated birds or dragons.

Undercroft The undercroft museum, created as a result of recent restoration work, traces the history of the city and its Minster, and among the remains from several different periods includes a fine reconstruction of a 4th-century wall painting; 10th-century grave slabs; a mid-10th-century shaft with excellent Scandinavian ornament; and early Norman capitals. The Treasury, also housed in the undercroft, contains a good collection of Yorkshire plate and York silver, as well as such treasures as the Horn of Ulf (an early-11th-century horn made from an elephant tusk and presented to the Minster as a symbol of a gift of land by a Viking thegn named Ulf).

Crypt Here part of Archbishop Roger's 12th-century work can be seen, surrounding the remnants of the original Norman choir. Notable is the font, with a modern cover by Sir Ninian Comper (**19**). Also on display is the 12th-century Doomstone, a Norman carving which shows hell as a mouth full of flames; in complete contrast is a delicately carved relief, also of the 12th century and rather Byzantine in appearance, of the Virgin and Child.

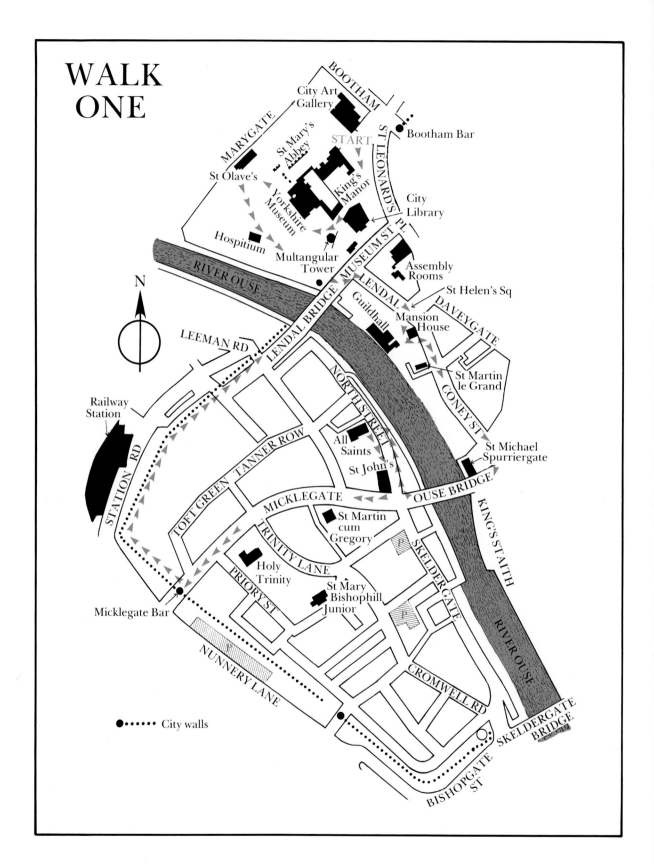

WALK ONE

BOOTHAM

City Art Gallery

Bootham Bar

MARYGATE

St Mary's Abbey

START

St Olave's

ST LEONARD'S PL.

King's Manor

City Library

Yorkshire Museum

Hospitium

Multangular Tower

MUSEUM ST

Assembly Rooms

St Helen's Sq

LENDAL

Guildhall

Mansion House

DAVEYGATE

N

RIVER OUSE

LEEMAN RD

LENDAL BRIDGE

St Martin le Grand

CONEY ST

Railway Station

STATION RD

TANNER ROW

NORTH STREET

All Saints

St John's

St Michael Spurriergate

OUSE BRIDGE

KING'S STAITH

TOFT GREEN

MICKLEGATE

St Martin cum Gregory

SKELDERGATE

RIVER OUSE

TRINITY LANE

Holy Trinity

PRIORY ST

St Mary Bishophill Junior

Micklegate Bar

NUNNERY LANE

CROMWELL RD

BISHOPGATE ST

SKELDERGATE BRIDGE

●••••• City walls

Three Walks through the City

Walk one: Exhibition Square to Micklegate Bar

Start in Exhibition Square outside the **City Art Gallery**. This was built to the designs of Edward Taylor for the Yorkshire Fine Art and Industrial Exhibition in 1879, and became the City Art Gallery in the 1890s. A major part of its small but interesting collection is the F. D. Lycett Green bequest of European old masters. The famous York artist Sir William Etty RA (1787–1849), who was born the son of a baker in Feasegate and whose statue stands in Exhibition Square, has a room devoted to his works. Many of his paintings are of nudes, for which this rather shy, gentle man was much criticised during his lifetime. There are also paintings by Van Dyck, Lely, Reynolds, Sickert, Stanley Spencer, Gwen John, Lowry and Paul Nash, and a collection of modern stoneware pottery.

As you face the Art Gallery the **King's Manor (20)** is to your left. This was originally the residence of the Abbot of St Mary's Abbey (parts of the foundations are 13th century); after the dissolution of the monasteries it became the headquarters of the Council of the North and residence of the Lord President (1538). Its name derives from its being the king's property, rather than from its having been a royal residence, though Henry VIII and Catherine Howard may have stayed in it in 1541, and over the main entrance is the royal coat of arms of Charles I, who stayed here in 1636 and 1639, when he moved the royal court to York. The monogram of his father, James I, who lodged here on his way from Scotland to London to assume the English crown, can also be seen on the doorway. To the right is another elaborate doorway, and there are more in the courtyard within.

Now part of the University of York, the King's Manor was put to a variety of uses after the disbanding of the Council of the North in 1641: as a private residence, divided into tenements, converted into a girls' school, and, from 1835, as the home of the Yorkshire School for the Blind, when the headmaster's house was built, designed by Walter Brierley. Parts of the building are open to the public, including the fine Huntingdon Room, in the north wing, which was part of a reconstruction by Henry Hastings, Earl of Huntingdon (Lord President 1572–95). The room has a most impressive plaster frieze and an unusual chimneypiece.

The frieze incorporates a Tudor royal badge (pomegranate and wyverns), the crest of the Hastings family (bull's head) and the badge of the Earls of Warwick, into whose family Henry Hastings married (bear with ragged staff). The chimneypiece has a striking design of radiating segments.

Turn sharp right on leaving the King's Manor and follow a narrow lane alongside it to the Museum Gardens. On the left is part of St Mary's Abbey boundary wall, erected in 1266; a wall once surrounded the entire abbey precincts, an area of 12 acres. Just beyond and above this runs the city wall, leading to the 10-sided **Multangular Tower** (**2**), which was built *c*300 – probably the finest visible remains of Roman York. The path diverges to the left for a good view of the interior. The work is Roman to a height of 19 ft (6.2 m), including the characteristic ornamental red tile band, while the upper 11 ft (3.3 m), with cruciform arrow slits in each of the tower's faces, is 13th century. The main path continues into the Museum Gardens.

20 *The mellow brickwork of the King's Manor. Originally the residence of the Abbot of St Mary's, it was rebuilt as the headquarters of the Council of the North during the 16th and 17th centuries. The doorways shown here date from 1610; over the one on the left is the coat of arms of Charles I, who stayed here in 1636 and 1639.*

21 *The architect of the Yorkshire Museum, William Wilkins, pioneered the Greek Revival in Britain (he also designed London's National Gallery), and argued for the Doric style in this instance on the grounds that 'you have such Gothic at York that any design in the same style must appear trifling'. Most of the building work and interior detail was supervised by R. H. Sharp and J. P. Pritchett. The Museum houses interesting collections relating to the geology and early history of York and the surrounding countryside.*

The **Yorkshire Museum** (**21**) was built for the Yorkshire Philosophical Association, a body whose formation in 1823 was inspired by the discovery of the Kirkdale fossils. The building was designed by the well-known architect of the Greek Revival movement, William Wilkins. First opened in 1830, it houses a splendid collection of artefacts relating to the geology, archaeology and early history of York and the surrounding area. Especially good is the Roman collection, which includes the famous head of Constantine (who was declared Emperor in York), a statue of Mars and some excellent mosaics. There are also finds from the Anglo-Saxon and Viking periods, notably the Ormside Bowl (an 8th-century ecclesiastical vessel richly decorated in silver gilt) and the 9th-century Gilling Sword. There is also a good collection of 18th- and 19th-century Yorkshire pottery. In the basement are medieval masonry fragments from St William's shrine (formerly in the Minster) and from St Mary's Abbey, among them superb sculptures of Moses, John the Baptist, and the Apostles.

According to tradition, **St Mary's Abbey** was first founded by Stephen of Lastingham, a monk of Whitby, *c*1080. It was given more land and virtually refounded by William Rufus in 1088, and became the wealthiest and most important Benedictine abbey in northern England. In 1132, 13 of its monks, believing the standards to be too lax, seceded from the abbey, and founded the Cistercian Abbey of Fountains (**55**). Although St Mary's lay outside the city, within its own precincts, there were frequent disputes with the city authorities about its rights, sometimes erupting in violence. The ruins that can be seen today (**22**) are mainly remnants of the grand and highly elaborate abbey church, 350 ft (107 m) long, built *c*1270: the outer walls of the north nave aisle (seen to particular advantage from outside the Museum), part of the west front, and some of the tower courses of the piers and walls of the south side. The church must have been one of the finest ecclesiastical buildings of its time. Soon after its dissolution, the abbey was used as a quarry, and its stones were put to such diverse uses as the repair of Beverley Minster and the construction of the County Gaol. Nowadays the abbey ruins make a deeply impressive setting, every three or four years, for the performance of the York Mystery Plays (see above, p. 18–19).

Go out through the abbey gatehouse, which contains 12th-century masonry in its outer arch and the remains of the vaulting, and turn right to the attractive church of **St Olave Marygate** (**23**). This was founded *c*1050 by Siward, Earl of Northumbria; it was given to Stephen of Lastingham as the nucleus of his monastery, but was soon replaced as the abbey's church, and began to serve parishioners outside the abbey walls. During the Civil War it was used as a platform for guns, and suffered severe damage in consequence (it was not repaired until 1721–2). The chancel was rebuilt in 1879; its east window contains medieval glass showing the Annunciation and (fourth light) St Olave. The churchyard, in which the artist Sir William Etty is buried, affords another view of the abbey ruins.

23 *The tower of St Olave's, in Marygate, seen from the Museum Gardens. This church witnesses to York's Scandinavian heritage; founded in the 11th century by the Danish Earl Siward, it is dedicated to the patron saint of Norway.*

22 *The ruins of the church of the Benedictine Abbey of St Mary, begun by Abbot Simon de Warwick in 1270 and probably complete by 1300. This view is of the nave north aisle wall, looking towards the north-west pier of the crossing.*

Return through the **Museum Gardens (24)**. The Yorkshire Philosophical Association laid the area out as botanical gardens in the early 19th century, and they are well maintained today, with peacocks strutting about among the carefully labelled plants and trees. Bear right, down the slope, to the Hospitium, once the abbey guest house. The ground floor was built *c*1310, while the timber-framed first floor dates from 1420 (it has been restored several times). At one end are the remains of the Watergate (two archways and a window above). The way out of the Gardens into Museum Street leads past the little astronomical observatory of 1831–3, restored and open to the public during the summer.

24 *The Museum Gardens, laid out to a design by Sir John Murray Naesmith, provide a peaceful retreat from the bustle of the nearby city centre.*

25 *A view of the Guildhall across the River Ouse; medieval in appearance, it is actually a reconstruction (1958–61) of the original (1446–8), which was destroyed during an air raid in 1942. In the Middle Ages this was where all the magnesian limestone for the building of the Minster, quarried 9 miles away at Tadcaster and brought here by river, was unloaded at the Watergate.*

Across the road in Lendal – the name is a corruption of St Leonard's Landing – the imposing house set back on the left, now a hotel, is still known as the **Judge's Lodging**, because from 1802 it served as the residence of the Assize judge. It was built for Dr C. Winteringham in 1720, on the site of the former churchyard of St Wilfrid; over the doorway can be seen a stone head representing Aesculapius, the god of healing.

Further along on the right, at the corner of St Helen's Square, an archway opens onto a narrow passage leading down to the **Guildhall (25)**. A Guildhall in York is first recorded in 1256, and the first mention of one on this site dates from 1378. Rebuilding was undertaken in 1446 at the joint expense of the Mayor and city, and the Master and Brethren of St Christopher's Guild, who were to have use of it on certain occasions. Reduced to a shell by an air raid in 1942, the building has been reconstructed as an almost exact replica, the arch-braced roof with colourful bosses being supported by 12 huge pillars, each hewn from a single oak. But where Victorian stained glass used to fill the windows, there is now clear glass – apart from the west window, in which an imaginatively composed work by Harry Harvey illustrates scenes and figures from York past and present. In the tracery are men and women who helped the city's development, while the five lights depict architecture,

local military history, the city arms and civic processions, fairs and markets, and education and social life. The adjoining old Council Chamber escaped damage during the air raid, and retains its 15th-century roof and panelling.

The Praetorian Gate, the main entrance to the Roman fortress, was in St Helen's Square. The Coney Street corner is now occupied by the elegant **Mansion House** (**26**), the official residence of the Lord Mayor during his term of office. It was built 1725–30 (ten years before London's Mansion House), possibly to designs by William Etty (1675–1734), a local carpenter and architect who worked with Hawksmoor on the mausoleum at Castle Howard. The pretty railings and lamp-posts are of a slightly later date. The city coat of arms, five golden lions superimposed on a red cross, appears in the pediment, which is supported by four Ionic pilasters. Much of the interior is furnished in keeping with the period of the house; the fine state room and banqueting hall occupy the whole of the first floor.

Coney Street (a derivation from 'King's Street') was for hundreds of years one of York's most important thoroughfares; besides the Guildhall, Mansion House and St Martin's Church it contained several of the main coaching inns, including the George. Nowadays it is a major shopping street, and inevitably some of its character has been lost in rebuilding. The great clock (**27**) of the church of **St Martin le Grand**, overlooking passers-by, was first erected in 1668 (the present cast-iron brackets are 19th century). The 'Little Admiral' on the top used to rotate, so that his sextant followed the sun, but was put out of action during World War II by the bomb which largely destroyed what had been the most important and probably the most impressive parish church in York. However, St Martin's has been cleverly restored by the architect G. G. Pace, and is very sprucely kept. It now consists of the 15th-century tower (formerly the south-west tower), the 14th-century south aisle (dedicated as a shrine of remembrance to York citizens who lost their lives in the war) and south arcade, and the south part of the nave. Opposite the south door, by which one enters, is the largest and best window of any parish church in the city, which was fortunately removed for safekeeping at the beginning of the war. The 15th-century glass, in strong tones of red, white and blue, depicts scenes from the life of St Martin of Tours; the donor of the window, Robert Semer, vicar of the church, is shown kneeling in homage, at the foot of the middle light. The church also contains a handsome 18th-century font cover with scrolly gilding; some good modern stained glass, particularly the east window, by Harry Stammers, which shows the burning of the church; and a unique hanging organ, a gift to the church from the German government and Evagelical church.

St Michael Spurriergate, further along on the right at the junction with Low and High Ousegate, has a rather dull exterior, the result of its outer walls being rebuilt in 1821, when it was shortened; but the interior, restored with great sensitivity by G. G. Pace in 1965, is a delight. The arcades are late Norman, with quatrefoil piers and waterleaf capitals which were retained when the arches themselves were heightened and the clerestory added in the 15th century; remarkably, the 15th-century west tower piers faithfully copy them. The church contains some

26 The festive pilastered and pedimented façade of the Mansion House (1725–30), residence of the Lord Mayor during his year of office. Here the city regalia and insignia are also housed. The sword of state was presented by Richard II in 1389, when he came to the city to settle a dispute; he took the sword he was wearing and gave it to the Mayor, granting him and his successors the title Lord Mayor in perpetuity. A charter of 1396 gave permission for the sword to be carried point upward in the presence of any of the noblemen of England.

27 *The 'Little Admiral' on the clock of St Martin le Grand church, taking sightings along his sextant, has been in position over Coney Street since 1778.*

28 *Looking back across the river near the Ouse Bridge to King's Staith, York's most important riverside quay since the Middle Ages. The name meant 'king's landing place', and may refer to royal visits in the 14th century. The whitewashed building on the left, the King's Arms inn, dates from the early 17th century; Cumberland House, on the right, was built in the early 18th century for William Cornwall, Lord Mayor.*

fine fittings, notably an early-18th-century reredos, exquisitely carved communion rails of the same period, and an extremely rare 15th-century brass of a chalice, in the floor to the north of the altar. The excellent stained glass includes a charming 15th-century window of the nine orders of angels in the south aisle, and part of a Jesse window. St Michael is now a healthfood café.

The three-arch **Ouse Bridge** was designed by Peter Atkinson the Younger (c1776–1843) and built between 1810 and 1821. There has long been a bridge on or near this site – certainly there was one here in 1154, which collapsed when huge crowds assembled to welcome back Archbishop William from his enforced retirement (engineered by jealous rivals) in Winchester. That no one was killed in this accident was regarded as his first and greatest miracle. He died soon after, reputedly poisoned by a resentful archdeacon, and in 1227 he was canonised, following reports of miracles occurring at his tomb in the Minster. The bridge was replaced by one of stone, which was covered with buildings that included the Council Chamber, a civil prison, and a chapel dedicated to St William. During the winter of 1564–5 the Ouse flooded and carried away the central pillar and two arches. The bridge was subsequently rebuilt as a single bow, making it at that time one of the longest in Europe (81 ft, 24.5 m), much to the wonder of the many visitors to the city.

On the far side of the bridge turn right into North Street. Opposite the huge and rather ugly Viking Hotel is one of the most attractive churches in York, **All Saints North Street**. Its core is late 12th century and some of its masonry is Roman, but the prevailing style is that of the 15th century,

when the north and south aisles were extended and the tall tapering spire was added. The chancel and chancel aisle roofs are thronged with carved angels. All Saints is especially famous for its stained glass (**29**), some of the best in the city outside the Minster. The 14th-century east window was given by members of the Blackburn family, who appear kneeling and surrounded by the Trinity, while above are figures of John the Baptist, St Anne teaching the Virgin to read, and St Christopher. In the north aisle the great 'Pricke of Conscience' window of *c*1410 illustrates the events of the last 15 days of the world (flood, earthquake, fire, stars falling from heaven etc.) as narrated in the 14th-century poem of the same name; it may be the work of John Thornton, glass-painting master of the Minster east window. The 'Corporal Acts of Mercy' window (see St Matthew) is of the same date. In the lower right-hand corner of the glowing nine orders of angels window in the south aisle a man is shown wearing spectacles, a most uncommon sight in medieval times. To the north of All Saints is a delightful row of late-15th-century timber-framed cottages.

Retracing your steps and turning right into **Micklegate**, you come on the right to the small church of **St John Micklegate**, mainly 14th and 15th century and internally altered to accommodate first the Institute of Advanced Architectural Studies and now the York Arts Centre. The half-timbered belfry was constructed in 1646, a rare example of building in York under Parliamentary rule.

Micklegate, the great main street of York, has been important for centuries, for it was part of the major route between London and Scotland, leading to the only bridge across the Ouse. Since the Middle Ages many of York's leading citizens have lived here; being close to the quays it was favoured by merchants, and during the 18th century the county's leading families tended to choose it for their town residences. Much of the street's Georgian character has been retained, enhanced by its gradual rise and curve. Note especially Garforth House (Nos. 52–4), built for Edmund Garforth in 1757; Bathurst House (No. 86 – the third storey was added *c*1820–5); and what is probably the finest house in the street, Micklegate House (Nos. 88–90), built in 1753, most likely by John Carr, for the Bourchier family. At the end of the 19th century it fell into disrepair, and for a time was used as a warehouse, many of its excellent fittings, being sold (some are in the Treasurer's House; see below, p. 81). It now belongs to the University, and has been much restored (**8**).

On the left before you reach these houses, standing in its leafy churchyard, is the church of **St Martin cum Gregory**, now used as the Diocesan Youth Office, but still containing much of interest. The building is mainly 13th–15th centuries, but the tower plinth is made of Roman stones from the Temple of Mithras which stood opposite the gate. Several of the windows contain medieval glass: two 15th-century panels, of the Betrayal and of David and Goliath, in the south chancel window; the east window (*c*1340), whose central panel shows St Martin of Tours dividing his cloak with the beggar; and the figures of John the Baptist and St Catherine, *c*1335, in the north aisle. Also in the north aisle, scratched on the plain glass inserted not long after the Jacobite Rebellion of 1745, can be read such loyalist sentiments as 'I hope this may be a plase for true protestants to resort to & never to be ruled by Papists God Bless

29 *All Saints North Street: reset 14th-century glass in the south aisle east window, showing the Virgin, the Crucifixion and St John. All Saints has perhaps the most interesting early stained glass of any parish church in York, a city renowned for the wealth and quality of its medieval glass.*

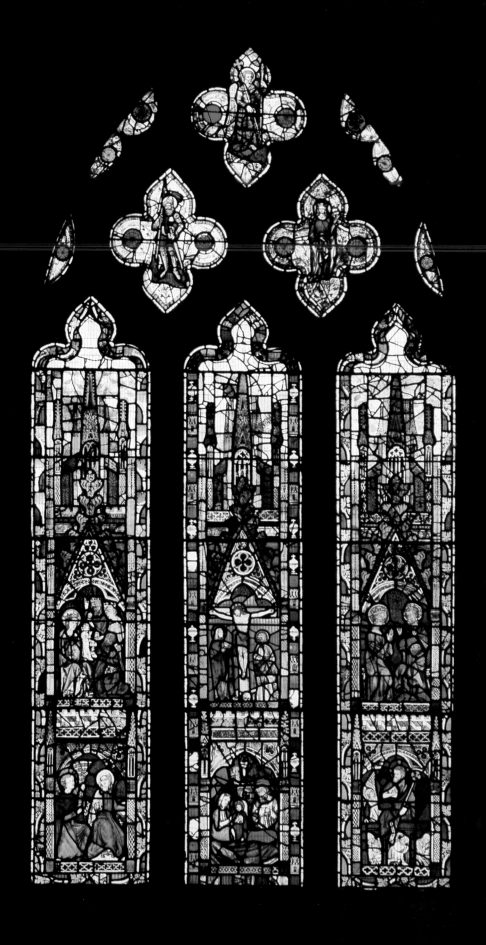

King George ye 2d & Billy off Cumberland Whome God long preserve'. The fittings include an 18th-century reredos made by a joiner, Bernard Dickinson, bread shelves in a decorative niche of the same date, and a 17th-century pulpit. Two noted York glass painters are buried in St Martin's, William Peckitt (1731–95) in the chancel and Henry Gyles (1645–1709) in the churchyard. Until the 19th century the Butter Market was held outside the church; all butter produced in the surrounding area had to be brought here to be 'viewed, searched, weighed and sealed'.

It is worth turning left off Micklegate, down Trinity Lane, to see **Jacob's Well**, a small timber-framed house with an intriguing 15th-century canopied porch of a type once common in York. This is now the only surviving example, and was brought here from a house in Daveygate. Trinity Lane takes its name from the large church just beyond it in Micklegate, **Holy Trinity**. This was formerly part of a priory founded in 1089 by Ralph Pagnell and attached to the Abbey of Marmoutier, near Tours. Badly damaged in the fire that devastated York in 1137, it was rebuilt between the end of the 12th century and the middle of the 13th. At the dissolution of the priory the church became parochial (1538). In 1552 the tower collapsed, bringing down the chancel; the present tower, the only external survival of the medieval fabric, was that of St Nicholas, the adjoining church. Restoration in the 19th century included a new chancel (1886) and rebuilding of the west front and porch (1902–5). The interior is chiefly notable for the fine 13th-century arcade, while the original triforium survives at the west end (the church was formerly

31 *Micklegate Bar, looking towards Micklegate: the traditional point of entry to the city for the sovereigns of England. In 1971, when York celebrated its 1900th anniversary, the Queen and the Duke of Edinburgh arrived here in procession, heralded (like earlier monarchs) by trumpeters posted on the Bar. The figures of knights holding stones, facing away from the city on the parapet, are replacements (1950) of the original ones, which were meant to ward off danger. Similar watchful or threatening figures face outward from the top of Monk Bar and Bootham Bar. The shields on the Bar include the arms of the city (to either side) and (above the arch) those of Sir John Lister-Kaye, Lord Mayor at the time of the restoration work carried out in 1737.*

30 *The ancient stocks in the churchyard of Holy Trinity Micklegate.*

32 The National Railway Museum, in the former York North Motive Power Depot, is one of the city's most popular attractions. The oldest locomotive on display is the Shutt End Colliery 0–4–0 'Agenoria' of 1829, a contemporary of Stephenson's 'Rocket', but perhaps the most famous is the LNER 4–6–2 Class A4 'Mallard', which set the still unbroken world steam speed record (126 mph) in the year it was made, 1938. Rolling stock displayed includes the sumptuous private coaches of Queen Adelaide and Queen Victoria. The steam locomotive shown here is the London Brighton and South Coast Railway Class A tank 'Boxhill' (1880), of a type that earned the nickname 'Rooters' or 'Terriers' by being small but very hardworking.

much higher); the 16th-century roof incorporates timberwork of an earlier period. On the south wall of the chancel is a memorial to Dr John Burton, historian and model for Dr Slop in Sterne's *Tristram Shandy*, with two volumes of his *Monasticon Eboracense* perched above him. It was outside the priory's gateway (demolished in the 1850s) that the medieval performances of the Mystery Plays used to begin. There are still some stocks in the churchyard (**30**).

Continue along Micklegate to **Micklegate Bar** (**31**), pausing for the view back down the street. The outer arch and passageway of this Bar date from the early 12th century, while the royal coat of arms indicates a late-14th-century date for the upper parts. The arms of the Lord Mayor Sir John Lister Kaye commemorate its restoration in 1737, and Peter Atkinson the Younger rebuilt the inner façade in 1827. The barbican had been demolished in the previous year, despite Sir Walter Scott's offer to walk from Edinburgh to York to save it. Until the 18th century this was the favourite place for displaying the heads of those who had been executed – as Shakespeare records: in his *Henry VI* Queen Margaret condemns the Duke of York with the words 'Off with his head, and set it on York gates, / So York may overlook the town of York.'

At this point it is possible to mount the **city walls**, and walk in either direction. If you bear north and north-west (right, looking from Micklegate), you come to Thomas Prosser's fine **Railway Station** of 1877. This was the second station to be built in York; the previous one, within the city walls at Toft Green, opened in 1841 but quickly proved inadequate for the growing volume of traffic. The outside of the present station, of rather dull Scarborough brick, belies its breathtaking interior (**11**): the great curved train shed, 800 ft (244 m) long, its roof girders radiating from Corinthian columns, is one of the glories of Victorian railway architecture. The spandrels of the cast-iron arches are filled with the coats of arms of the three main companies that amalgamated to form the North Eastern Railway in 1853.

The importance of York as a centre of Britain's railway network makes it a highly appropriate place for the **National Railway Museum** (Leeman Road), probably the major museum of its kind in the world. It combines the collections of the former British Transport Museum at Clapham, London, and the LNER Museum in York, and is housed in the old York North Motive Power Depot, which has been skilfully converted to suit its new purpose. The main display, in the Great Hall, covers nearly 2 acres; here engines and rolling stock of innumerable types and periods can be seen, in beautiful condition and with highly informative labels (**32**). A series of galleries contains smaller items and special exhibitions relating to the railway world, and there is an art gallery showing 19th- and 20th-century paintings and posters. A schoolboy's dream come true, it appeals to schoolboys and girls of all ages.

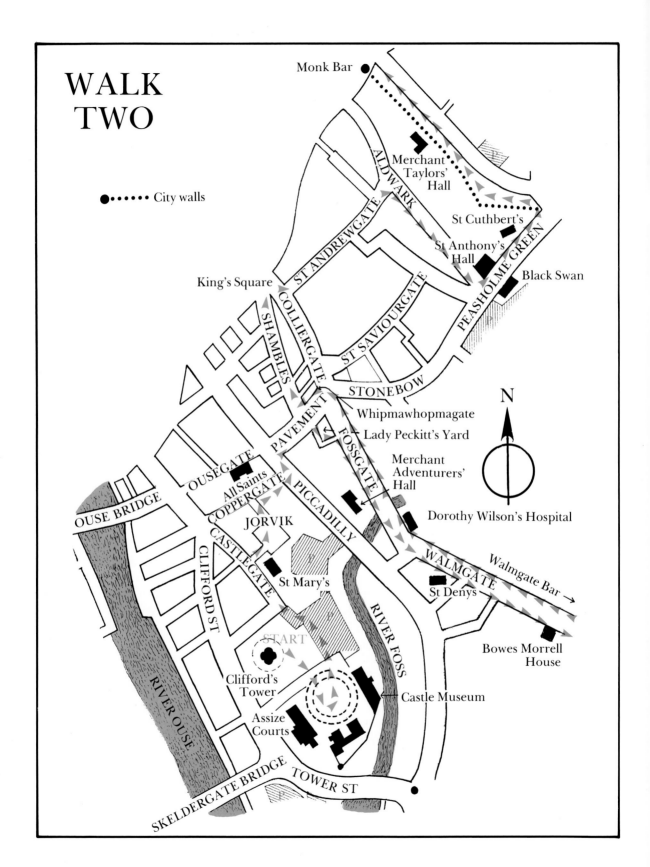

WALK TWO

Monk Bar

●······ City walls

King's Square

ALDWARK

ST ANDREWGATE

Merchant Taylors' Hall

St Cuthbert's

St Anthony's Hall

PEASHOLME GREEN

Black Swan

COLLIERGATE

SHAMBLES

ST SAVIOURGATE

STONEBOW

Whipmawhopmagate

Lady Peckitt's Yard

N

PAVEMENT

FOSSGATE

Merchant Adventurers' Hall

OUSEGATE

All Saints

COPPERGATE

PICCADILLY

Dorothy Wilson's Hospital

OUSE BRIDGE

JORVIK

CASTLEGATE

CLIFFORD ST

St Mary's

WALMGATE

St Denys

Walmgate Bar →

RIVER FOSS

RIVER OUSE

START

Clifford's Tower

Bowes Morrell House

Castle Museum

Assize Courts

SKELDERGATE BRIDGE

TOWER ST

Walk two: Clifford's Tower to Bootham Bar

Clifford's Tower (33) and the remains of the medieval curtain wall are all that survives nowadays of **York Castle**. Founded by William the Conqueror in 1068, it was destroyed by English and Danish rebels the following year but immediately rebuilt. The present stone tower, an elegant quatrefoil shape but now a roofless shell, dates from *c*1244–70 and was probably built under the direction of Master Henry de Reyns, who also worked on Westminster Abbey. It formed the keep of the new castle, and contained a chapel, a hall and other rooms. How it got its name is uncertain – in medieval documents it is referred to as 'the great tower'; it may be because the body of the rebellious Sir Richard Clifford was hanged on it in 1322, or because of the claim of the Clifford family, one of the most powerful in the north, to be its hereditary constables. One can go into Clifford's Tower and walk round the top: there is a fine view of St Mary Castlegate, All Saints Pavement and the Minster. On the way down, notice the chapel, originally mid 13th century with wall arcading of that date and restored in the 14th and 17th centuries. The upper part of the room formerly housed the portcullis mechanism of the tower.

Throughout the Middle Ages the castle, roughly lozenge-shaped and surrounded by a high wall and moat, was put to a variety of uses besides serving as a stronghold. When York was the centre of royal government, the king's court and treasure were housed here; it was used as a meeting place of the circuit courts; and it was a prison. From the mid 14th century the fabric began to deteriorate. Richard III seems to have intended some sort of major renovation, but in fact only succeeded in partly destroying it. In 1596 the gaoler, Robert Redhead, started to demolish Clifford's Tower and sell the stone; only the protestations of the City Corporation, who complained that they would have no 'other building for showe of this cittie, save but onlye the minster and church steeples, if the said towre should be pulled downe', ensured its preservation. It was never directly involved in hostilities, but in the siege of York it played a defensive role, and it continued to be garrisoned until 1684, when a fire set the magazine alight and blew up everything but the outer walls. An old tradition holds that the fire was started deliberately, for that night toasts were drunk in the city 'to the destruction of the Minced Pie' (as it was popularly known).

The centre of the bailey area has long been grassed, and since the 1790s has had at its centre an oval lawn known as 'the eye of the Ridings' (the Yorkshire counties). Here county elections for the whole of Yorkshire were held until 1832, and for the North Riding (now absorbed in the County of North Yorkshire) until 1882. This was also the scene of proclamations of the accession of monarchs, and declarations of war and peace; and, from 1802, of executions.

What used to be the main part of the bailey area of the castle is now occupied by three imposing 18th-century buildings facing Clifford's Tower. In the centre (looking from the tower) is the **Debtors' Prison** (1701–5), an impressive example of the English Baroque and clearly inspired by Vanbrugh and Hawksmoor. The architect is unknown, but may have been William Wakefield, the designer of various country houses to the north of York. Daniel Defoe described it as 'the most stately and complete prison of any kind in the kingdom, if not in Europe'. Conditions inside did not always match the grandeur of the exterior, indeed on several occasions prisoners died of suffocation in the over-crowded cells.

To the right are the **Assize Courts** (1773–7), designed by John Carr, with a grand Ionic elevation and recessed portico. In the pediment is a finely carved wreath and crossed fasces and a staff, the cap of liberty hanging from the end of the staff. Above stands the figure of Justice, bearing scales and a spear. The two splendid courtrooms, still regularly used, are each rectangular and crowned with a circular dome which rests on columns arranged in a square rather than a circle. To the left of the Debtors' Prison is the **Female Prison**, built in 1780 to the designs of Thomas Wilkinson and John Prince under Carr's supervision. The centre of the exterior is almost identical to that of the Assize Courts. The flanking pavilions were added in 1802 by Peter Atkinson the Elder.

Nowadays the Female Prison and the Debtors' Prison house the largest and most popular folk museum in the country, the **Castle Museum**. Its originator was Dr John Kirk, a country doctor from Pickering, who from the 1890s to the 1930s made a collection of everyday items that he saw passing out of use, as he travelled around the remote farms and villages of north Yorkshire. The innumerable objects have been continually added to since they were brought here from Memorial Hall, Pickering, in the 1930s, and they are all imaginatively displayed. There are meticulous reconstructions of rooms and of whole streets of different periods – perhaps the most famous of all is Kirkgate, a group of real 19th-century buildings and shopfronts set in a cobbled street, complete with hansom cab, to form a wonderfully atmospheric Victorian scene. Half Moon Court recreates an Edwardian street, again using original buildings, while Thornley Park evokes a park in an Edwardian industrial town. The Museum has excellent collections of farm implements, costumes and accessories, weapons and armour – in short, something to suit every taste, and well worth a leisurely visit. Among the most interesting of the recent acquisitions is a 7th-century warrior's helmet, found in nearby Coppergate.

Cross the carpark (the site of a 19th-century prison building demolished in 1935) to Castlegate, formerly the main road leading to the castle. Here is one of York's finest Georgian houses, **Fairfax House** (*c*1755–6), built for Viscount Fairfax by John Carr – the bands of stone marking the floors on the front of the building are typical of his work. The interior contains outstanding plasterwork and woodwork, and one of the grandest staircases in the city. It has been restored by the York Civic Trust, and the Terry Collection of Georgian furniture is installed there. On the other side of the street is another house by Carr, **Castlegate House** (**34**), built in 1759 for the City Recorder, Peter Johnson.

The fabric of **St Mary Castlegate** dates mainly from the 15th century, when the church was remodelled and extended, but there are remains of 12th-century work in the north aisle. During restoration under Butterfield in 1868–70, an early-11th-century foundation stone was discovered, inscribed to the effect that a church called a 'mynster' was founded by Efrard, Grim and Aese; but its links with this church have not been

33 *Standing on the motte of William the Conqueror's castle is Clifford's Tower, a keep rebuilt in stone at the instigation of Henry II in 1244. In design it is one of the largest and most advanced towers of its date, unusual in its quatrefoil shape. It contained a hall, and had a chapel over the entrance. It seems to have been strongly defended – arrow slits and gun ports can be seen in the outer walls. However, much of its life was spent in a state of disrepair; in 1360 it was described as cracked from top to bottom, and the huge crack is still visible (to the right of the side shown here), with an infill of differently coloured stone.*

definitely proved. St Mary Castlegate has now been converted to house the 'York Story', which, by means of audio-visual aids – slide shows, tableaux, tapestries, recordings – gives an introduction to the city's development over the past 1900 years, especially its social and architectural history. Designed by James Gardner and opened in 1975, the 'York Story' formed the city's contribution to the European Architectural Heritage Year.

Another and more special evocation of the distant past is to be found in St Mary's Square at the **Jorvik Viking Centre**, opened by Prince Charles in May 1984 after five years of excavation in this area by the York Archaeological Trust. It lies under the Coppergate shopping precinct, and uses the latest technology to present history in an entirely new way. The visitor steps aboard a remote-controlled car and is 'transported back in time' to Viking-age York, travelling through Coppergate (the street of the coopers or cupmakers) as it would then have appeared, passing close-packed houses and workshops built of wattle and thatch, watching figures busy at work or carrying out everyday tasks in the street and in their homes, hearing the sounds and even smelling the smells of 9th-century Jorvik. At the end of their vivid journey visitors can see a reconstruction of the dig in progress, and some of the original timbers of the houses that were unearthed; in places these had survived to shoulder height, and are by far the best preserved of their period in the country. It has been possible to show from them that their layout influenced all subsequent property divisions in York, even to the present day.

Up Coppergate Walk is one of York's most famous churches, **All Saints Pavement** (**35**), easily recognisable by its lantern tower with a tall openwork top. This is a 19th-century reproduction of the original, whose light was supposed to have guided travellers to the city through the medieval Forest of Galtres; nowadays the light shines out after dusk as a memorial to the citizens who died in the two world wars. The church was rebuilt towards the end of the 14th century, when the north aisle seems to have been constructed out of the remains of the earlier structure; and in the late 18th century the chancel and chancel aisle were pulled down so that the market place could be enlarged. There are several interesting fittings: the 13th-century knocker on the north door in the form of a lion, representing hell, swallowing the head of a bearded man; the 15th-century lectern; a jolly painted pulpit with tester on a chalice base, made by Nicholas Hall in 1634; the Lord Mayor's tables in the south aisle, listing the parishioners who served as Lord Mayor; and a nicely worded memorial (1803) to Tate Wilkinson, the famous manager of the Theatre Royal. The west window, a rearrangement of richly coloured glass (c1370) brought here from the church of St Saviour, relates episodes from the Passion. All Saints has strong connections with the city guilds. In January the annual service of the Merchant Adventurers' Company is held here, in accordance with the will (1692) of Jane Stainton, a merchant's wife, which also stipulates that the sermon preached on the occasion should 'exhort the members to think upon their latter end'. The Guild of York Freemen also have their annual service here, in April; they process to the church from their Court Room in St William's College, dressed in green and red robes.

34 *Castlegate House was designed by the well-known York architect John Carr for Peter Johnson, City Recorder 1759–89, at the beginning of his term of office. It is one of Carr's most attractive town houses (another fine example, Fairfax House, stands almost opposite). Above the doorway shown here the windows of the first floor are crowned with a distinctive series of round-headed arches derived from Robert Adam, with whom Carr worked at Harewood House (see p. 90).*

Pavement was one of York's two principal market places (the other was Thursday Market, now renamed St Sampson's Square). Its name, presumably meaning a metalled or paved area, was first recorded *c*1329; prior to that it is referred to in documents as Marketshire. It was the scene of public gatherings, executions and lesser punishments (the pillory was sited here). Its appearance has been considerably altered since medieval times by the creation of Parliament Street (1836) and Piccadilly (1912). On the right-hand side is the finely timbered **Herbert House** (*c*1620), one of the few early-17th-century houses in York. It takes its name from the family of Christopher Herbert, a merchant and Lord Mayor of the city, who bought a house on this site in 1557. His great-grandson, who was probably born in nearby Lady Peckitt's Yard, was Gentleman of the Bedchamber to Charles I, and attended the king at his execution.

Lady Peckitt's Yard, the narrow alley to the right of Herbert House, is named after the wife of John Peckitt, Lord Mayor 1702–3 (it used to be said in York that while the Mayor was 'a Lord for a year and a day, his wife is a Lady for ever and aye'). Its narrowness and overhanging houses give a good idea of what the city's streets looked like in former centuries; there is even a wing built right across the alley. After becoming much less picturesque it leads into Fossgate, which was one of the wealthiest parishes in the Middle Ages and the home of many rich merchants. Across the street is the former Electric Theatre (now Macdonalds), a remarkable terracotta edifice (1911) with a 'Venetian' façade on a giant scale.

We turn right, however, through the archway (**36**) leading to the **Merchant Adventurers' Hall**. Founded in 1357 as a religious institution, the Guild of Our Lord and the Blessed Virgin, and given a licence by Edward III to form a fraternity and hold property, the company came to be dominated by the mercers and played a signal role in the commercial life of the city, especially in the early 15th century, when the cloth trade was at its peak. A building seems to have been constructed for the guild soon after its formation, but most of the present fabric is characteristically 15th century, notably the oak roof trusses of the massive timber-framed Great Hall (the panelling here is Elizabethan, while the windows were inserted in the 18th century to give more light). The Hall is decorated with portraits and banners, and is still used for traditional court meetings and feasts. The oldest part of the building is the undercroft, dating from the mid 14th century. Until the 19th century it was used as a hospital for poverty-stricken members of the company, being divided into sleeping and sitting rooms for five men and five women. At the far end of the undercroft is the Trinity Chapel, built in 1368 and restored in 1411. It is now very simple and austere, an evocative example of late-17th-century plainness, with clear glazed windows, late-17th-century seating and a pulpit of the same date dominating the chapel from the east end. Virtually the only decoration is the coat of arms of Charles II on the north wall and of the Merchant Adventurers of England on the south wall. The other rooms in the hall are filled with a variety of interesting furniture, much of it 17th-century English oak; note especiallly the large late-16th-century Abbot's chair in the room before the Governor's Parlour,

35 All Saints Pavement: part of the west window, containing late-14th-century glass formerly in St Saviour Saviourgate that interestingly illustrates a new vitality in York glass painting of this period. Very little glass was installed in the second part of the 14th century, most likely because of the havoc wrought by the Black Death. This window depicts 12 scenes from Christ's Passion, and its emphasis on this rather than on earlier parts of His life is also possibly due to the lasting influence of the plague. The panels shown here, in the lower left and centre of the window, are of the Marys and the angel at the tomb, Christ's appearance to Mary Magdalene, His appearance to St Thomas, and a figure under a canopy (a composite panel of reset glass).

and the company's pretty 18th-century mace, still used on formal occasions, in the parlour itself. On leaving, go round to the front facing Piccadilly to admire the wealth of exposed timbering.

Back in Fossgate, cross the River Foss (which flows into the Ouse south of the castle) by Peter Atkinson the Younger's charming humpbacked bridge, designed in 1811 and little altered since. Here Fossgate becomes Walmgate. Immediately on the left is **Dorothy Wilson's Hospital** (1812),

36 *The gatehouse of the Merchant Adventurers' Hall in Fossgate. The frontage seen here is an almost exact reconstruction of the 17th-century entrance.*

named after the lady who endowed it (1717) for the maintenance of ten poor women, and for the instruction of 20 poor boys in 'English, reading and writing'. In the 19th century Walmgate was a notorious area of slum dwellings and acute poverty, and it is still rather depressing, but it has some rewards for the church architecture enthusiast who undertakes the walk up and down it, and it leads to the city's most complete gateway. The less energetic should turn back to Pavement (see below).

The church of **St Denys**, on the right as one goes down Walmgate, presents a rather truncated appearance, for the nave and spire were demolished in 1798, and there was further reconstruction (e.g. of the tower) in the 19th century. The beautiful Norman south doorway has four recessed orders decorated with beakheads, carved foliage and chevron ornament. Most of the surviving building is of *c*1330–40, with reticulated window tracery and thin, closely set buttresses. The north aisle windows have exceptionally fine 14th-century glass, including a tree of Jesse, while the westernmost window contains two medallions that are possibly 12th century and certainly amongst the oldest glass in York. In the east window is 15th-century glass (**37**), a fragmentary Crucifixion and St Denys carrying his head. A monument to Dorothy Wilson, in the shape of a Georgian door, recounts her many charities, and there is also an ornate Jacobean memorial to Dorothea Hughes.

Further along Walmgate on the left is **St Margaret's**, now set rather forlornly in a large churchyard surrounded by modern buildings. Apart from the tower (1684) the church was mostly rebuilt 1851–2, but it has a superb 12th-century barrel-vaulted porch, brought here from St Nicholas, Hull Road, after the siege of 1644. The outer arch is supported on four shafts, each carved in a bold zig-zag, as though the stonemason had decided to concertina straight shafts; the inner has three orders with richly carved capitals. The voussoirs of the arches are carved too, and the door jambs are shafted, with capitals. Heads, mythological figures, animals and signs of the zodiac appear in the carving.

Along the street on the opposite side notice the late-14th-century timber-framed **Bowes Morrell House**, an early example of domestic building; it was restored in 1966 by the York Civic Trust, who have done so much to preserve historic buildings in the city. **Walmgate Bar** (**38**) is the only one to preserve its barbican, and it also still has its portcullis (the lower spikes can be seen poking down from the roof of the arch) and 15th-century gates.

Most of the structure is 14th century, though it was badly damaged during the siege and subsequently repaired. The wood and plaster buildings on the inner side are Elizabethan.

Retracing our steps up Fossgate we turn left into Pavement, and facing us is **Whipmawhopmagate**, the shortest street in York, with the longest name. Its curious title may indicate that this was the place where criminals were whipped, or it may be a derivation from the dialect words 'whitna whatna', meaning 'what kind of?'. It was formerly bounded by one of York's finest medieval churches, St Crux (the Cross, not a saint), which was demolished in 1887. The parish room that now stands on the site incorporates a fragment of medieval wall and a traceried door, and contains an impressive collection of monuments.

OVERLEAF

37 (left) *The east window of St Denys Walmgate: 15th-century glass, restored in 1980, showing the Virgin, part of a Crucifixion, and one of the best figure panels in York, of a crowned king giving his hand to a bishop, watched by three interested spectators.*

38 (right) *Walmgate Bar has the only complete town's barbican in England. The parallel walls were built out at right angles to the city walls, ending in a gateway with a portcullis. This view, looking up the barbican from outside the walls, shows how efficient the defences must have been: any attackers who got through the gateway would still have had to force their way through this long narrow entry. Beyond, in Walmgate, the 14th-century Bowes Morrell House can be seen on the left.*

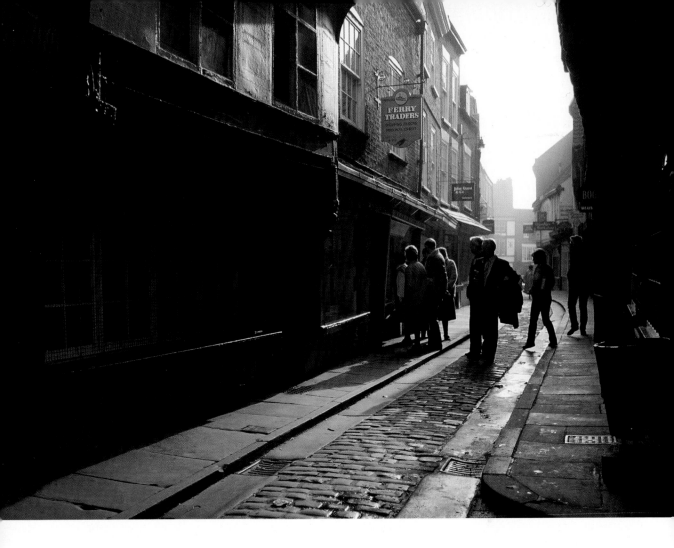

Whipmawhopmagate leads via a covered passage into the best known of all the streets in York, the **Shambles (39)**, whose name comes from the 'shamnels', the stalls or benches on which meat was displayed – for butchers have been associated with this street for hundreds of years. Today only one butcher is left, but there are many leather workers, continuing something of the Shambles' traditions. Most of the shops sell craft goods, antiques and souvenirs to the thousands of visitors who flock here, and in some the meat hooks and shelves have been kept as a reminder of the past. The 14th- and 15th-century overhanging houses and cobbled street are certainly picturesque, and although most of its buildings have been much restored, the Shambles gives a good impression of the shape of a medieval street. On the left, at No. 35, is a shrine dedicated to Margaret Clitherow, a butcher's wife who was cruelly pressed to death in 1586 for harbouring Jesuit priests – a fate which she suffered nobly, and for which she was canonised St Margaret of York in 1970. She is traditionally believed to have lived in this house, but recent research makes a much stronger case for one on the opposite side of the street.

Bear right across the pleasant open space of **King's Square (40)**. This was probably the site of the palace of the Danish kings, and was definitely that of the Roman Porta Principalis Sinistra, the gate on the left side of

39 The Shambles, one of York's most picturesque streets, made so narrow by its overhanging upper storeys that the sun never properly fills it. It is among the oldest thoroughfares in the city, being mentioned by name in the Domesday Book (1086). For many centuries it was the street of the butchers, whose benches for displaying meat, known as shamnels, gave the Shambles its name.

the fortress. At the far end of St Andrewgate we come to the **Merchant Taylors' Hall** in Aldwark. Its rather dreary brick exterior is a recasting of *c*1672 and *c*1715, and gives no hint of the exciting medieval interior, a 15th-century timber hall with an arch-braced roof (strengthened by later tie beams). Some of the stained glass in the outer room is by the famous York glass painter Henry Gyles. Next to the Hall stand the company's almshouses, built in 1730. The Merchant Taylors were first granted a charter in 1662, but a medieval guild of tailors was in existence by 1415.

Aldwark is an old English word meaning 'old fortification', and here it probably refers to a Roman one. The other notable buildings in the street are 18th century. Oliver Sheldon House, to the right of the Merchant Taylors' Hall, is well restored and has a handsome early Georgian front. At the far end of Aldwark is York's first Methodist chapel, a plain square building which was opened in 1759, when John Wesley himself conducted the service. Round to the right in St Saviour's Place is Peasholme House (**8**), originally built for or by a carpenter named Robert Heworth in 1752 and restored in 1975 by the York Civic Trust, whose label describes the house as being probably by John Carr.

Diagonally opposite, on Peasholme Green, is **St Anthony's Hall**, built for the religious and social Guild and Fraternity of St Anthony in the

40 *The pleasant open space of King's Square, amidst the narrow lanes in the centre of the city. Until 1937 the area was occupied by Christ Church and its churchyard. The houses in the background have 18th-century frontages on earlier structures. The square is first recorded as Konungsgarthr, King's Residence, and here the Northumbrian kings who ruled in the early Middle Ages are thought to have had their palace.*

41 *Monk Bar, which
commands the road to
the east, seen from
Goodramgate; this is
an ancient façade (the
first three floors are
14th century, the upper
stage 15th century),
and the only rear (i.e.
city-facing) side of any
of the major bars to
have been built
originally wholly in
masonry. The bars used
to be kept locked
between 9p.m. and
4a.m. every night, the
keys being held by
freemen who checked
on all traffic through
the gates. A ruling of
1463 laid down that
during the daytime
each bar was to be
guarded by two tall
men who would
interrogate suspicious
arrivals. The strict
watch was continued
through the 16th and
17th centuries, and
there was special
vigilance in times of
danger from epidemics
of plague.*

15th century. The ground floor is stone on two sides and brick on the other two, while on the upper floor brick has replaced the original timber framing. The main hall is on the upper floor and has a fine open timberwork roof with a number of splendid bosses. After the dissolution of the Guild in 1627, St Anthony's Hall was by turns an arsenal, a workhouse and a prison; in 1705 it became the home of the York Bluecoat School. Now it is used by the Borthwick Institute of Historical Research, part of the University.

The attractive black and white timber-framed **Black Swan** pub, on the other side of the street, was built in the late 16th century, and incorporates earlier framing in the south wall. This was once the family home of Sir Martin Bowes, who became goldsmith to Elizabeth I and Lord Mayor of London. He presented his native city with its sword of state, which is still carried in front of the Lord Mayor when he attends the monthly council meetings in the Guildhall. Later the house was lived in by the parents of General Wolfe, conqueror of French Canada. The Black Swan claims to be the oldest building in York used as an inn. It was Sir Martin Bowes' influence that saved the church of **St Cuthbert** (which we now pass as we turn left down Peasholme Green) when it was threatened with demolition in the 16th century. The building seems to be a 15th-century enlargement of an earlier structure, and part of the east wall bears the outline of a Saxon gable. The church is now the administrative centre of the parish of St Michael le Belfry.

At the end of Peasholme Green bear left and climb up the steps to the **city walls**. Immediately there is a superb view of the Minster. Follow the walk round to **Monk Bar (41)**, probably so named from a neighbouring monastery. The four-storey gatehouse dates from the early 14th century and was heightened during the 15th century. It is a very sophisticated piece of design; under attack it could act as a self-contained fortress, each floor being defensible even if the others had been captured. On the outer face is the royal coat of arms of the Plantagenets, and high up are the gallery holes through which missiles were shot. The inner face is the only medieval one to have survived. In the 16th century Monk Bar was used as the freemen's prison.

The walk along the walls from here to Bootham Bar is a must for every visitor, for it provides a continuous panorama of glorious views across attractively laid out gardens to the Minster, the back of the Treasurer's House (see below, p. 81), the elegant Georgian and neo-Georgian houses of the Minster precincts, and the remains of the **Bishop's Palace**. The walk is at tree-top level, and in summer there is the added richness of the scent of lime flowers. The best remaining section of the moat that once surrounded the city lies between the wall and Lord Mayors Walk below, and is said to be the best preserved ditch of its kind in England.

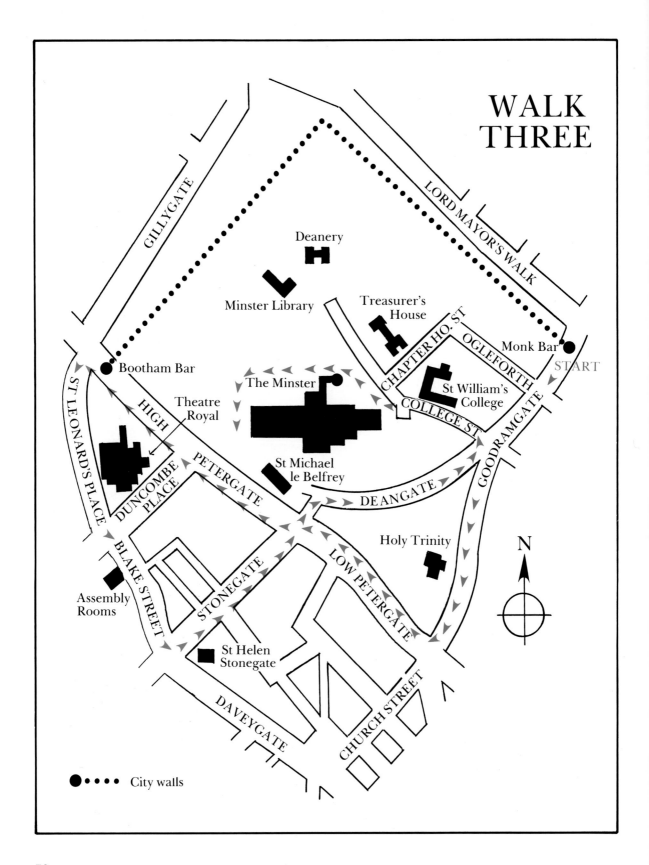

WALK THREE

Deanery

Minster Library

Treasurer's House

CHAPTER HO. ST

OGLEFORTH

Monk Bar

START

GILLYGATE

LORD MAYOR'S WALK

Bootham Bar

The Minster

St William's College

COLLEGE ST

GOODRAMGATE

ST LEONARD'S PLACE

HIGH

Theatre Royal

St Michael le Belfrey

DEANGATE

DUNCOMBE PLACE

PETERGATE

Holy Trinity

N

BLAKE STREET

STONEGATE

LOW PETERGATE

Assembly Rooms

St Helen Stonegate

CHURCH STREET

DAVEYGATE

●•••• City walls

Walk three: Monk Bar to the Minster

Having admired Monk Bar (see above, pp. 80–1), walk away from it up **Goodramgate** and turn right into Ogleforth to see the 17th-century house on the left, Cromwell House (1700) on the right, and the group of cottages with overhanging upper storeys on the corner with Chapter House Street. Goodramgate is an attractive curving street punctuated with craft and antique shops. Some of them preserve their half-timbering on the upper floors, but others unfortunately have modern additions not entirely in keeping with the street's character. On the right is one of the earliest surviving jettied ranges in the country, Our Lady's Row, a line of cottages built in 1316 to endow a chantry of the Virgin Mary at the adjacent church of Holy Trinity.

Holy Trinity, entered through a gateway of 1815 and a pretty little churchyard, is one of the most unspoilt and evocative churches in York, the only one really to retain an 18th-century atmosphere (having escaped the excesses of Victorian restoration). It was built between 1250 and 1500 on earlier foundations, and comprises a nave with north and south aisles and a south chapel. Notice the interlaced mouldings of the tower arch and the nave arcades. The original box pews, some Jacobean and some 18th century, are still in position, sitting unevenly on the delightfully undulating floor. The fine communion rails, the two-decker pulpit and the reredos with the Ten Commandments, Creed and Lord's Prayer written out are all of the period. Between the chapel and the main body of the church is a squint or hagioscope, through which the priest before the chapel altar could see the high altar. There is some good glass in the east window, dated 1472 and donated by the rector, John Walker. It shows, from the left, St George, St John the Baptist, the Holy Trinity, St John the Evangelist, and St Christopher, and, below, St Mary Cleopas and her family, St Anne and St Joachim with the Virgin and Child, the Coronation of the Virgin by the Trinity, Salome and Zebedee with St John the Evangelist as a child, and St Ursula. The tower of the church, built in the late 15th century, has a rare saddleback roof.

At the end of Goodramgate turn right into **Low Petergate**, which takes its name from the Minster, the Cathedral of St Peter (the distinction between High and Low Petergate was first made in 1736, but did not pass into common usage until the 19th century). The steeply gabled group of houses on the left makes a picturesque foreground to the view of the Minster towers at the top of the street – the characteristic York view. The street is on the line of the Via Principalis, one of the two main streets of the Roman fortress. It contains buildings of all ages, many of them now used as shops, while High Petergate (**42**) still has a more residential air. On the left in **High Petergate** is Guy Fawkes Tavern, which claims to be the birthplace of Guy Fawkes, caught on 5 November 1605 in his attempt, as one of a group of disaffected Catholics, to blow up the Houses of Parliament. It is actually more likely that he was born in nearby Stonegate, where his father owned property.

Opposite is the church of **St Michael le Belfry**, so called because of its proximity to the bell towers of the Minster. It was virtually rebuilt between 1525 and 1536, under the direction of master mason John

Forman, who also worked at the Minster, and it presents a more uniform appearance than many of the churches in the city. The interior, in late Gothic style, is an interesting example of Tudor ecclesiastical architecture (the west end was rebuilt at the end of the 19th century). It has the typical York rectangular plan, with a nave and two aisles. Much of the glass is 16th century, a rare period for glass in the city. The east window contains a collection of glass of 1330 from an earlier church. The panels in the centre row depict, from the left, St Peter and St Paul, the Annunciation, the Nativity, the Resurrection, and the Coronation of the Virgin. There are several good fittings, including the beautiful reredos (1712) carved by William Etty (the painting in the centre is a copy of the School of Velasquez *Adoration of the Shepherds*), elegant 18th-century communion rails, and the royal coat of arms of Queen Anne (on the gallery). The parish registers contain the entry 'Christeninges, 1570, Guye Fawke, sone to Edward Fawke the XVI day of Aprile'.

Cross the top of Duncombe Place, a wide thoroughfare formed in the 19th century to replace the narrow Lop Lane and give a better view of the west front of the Minster. It is named after a former Dean of the Minster, who subscribed £1000 to have it made. At the end of High Petergate stands **Bootham Bar** (**43**), on the site of the Roman Prima Porta Dextra, the entrance on the right side of the fortress. In medieval times this formed the main entrance to the city from the north through the Forest of Galtres, and armed guards were posted at it to guide travellers through the forest in safety and protect them from wild beasts. The late-11th-century outer arch is the oldest piece of post-Conquest masonry in

42 Looking up High Petergate in the direction of Duncombe Place. The site of the supposed (but very doubtful) birthplace of Guy Fawkes, of Gunpowder Plot fame, is now occupied by Youngs Hotel, a three-storey brick building constructed c1700 and considerably altered over the centuries, though at the back the original Dutch gables can still be seen. In a round-headed window between the first and second floors is some painted glass, depicting the arms of the city and the Hanoverian royal arms, signed Thomas Hodgson, 1801.

43 *Bootham Bar –
seen here from inside
the walls, looking up
High Petergate and
out into Bootham –
dominates the road to
the north, in the
Middle Ages the
direction from which
there was greatest
danger of attack. The
outer arch is late 11th
century, and contains
some of the oldest
masonry in the city
fortifications; this face
was rebuilt in stone in
1719 and refaced in
1835. In 1603 repairs
cost £10, including £4
for painting and
gilding (in preparation
for James 1's visit); in
1970, restoration cost
£25,000.*

the fortifications round the city, while the upper part of this front is mid 14th century, much altered and repaired. The inner face was rebuilt by Peter Atkinson the Younger in 1835, when he replaced a classical façade of 1719. The name, meaning the bar at the booths, first occurs in 1200; it was near here that the monks of St Mary's Abbey had the right to hold a weekly market.

Now bear left along **St Leonard's Place**. This takes its name from the great medieval Hospital of St Leonard, which occupied a large area of this part of the city in the Middle Ages. According to tradition it was founded by King Athelstan *c*937, but nothing certain is known about it until after 1066, when it was granted lands and a chapel dedicated to St Peter was built – apparently it was attached to the Minster in some way. The buildings were badly damaged by the great fire of 1137 and were rebuilt by King Stephen, who changed the Hospital's dedication to St Leonard. It became one of the largest and grandest of such institutions before being suppressed in 1539 by Henry VIII. Part of its buildings were used for the Royal Mint between 1546 and 1679. Today very little of it remains visible: a ruined building on the north-west side of Museum Street (probably part of the infirmary), and a 13th-century vaulted undercroft underneath the Theatre Royal.

The wide sweep of St Leonard's Place contains the only neoclassical terrace in York (**45**). It was designed by John Harper, and the contemporary railings were made by the Walker Iron Foundry. On the left are the De Grey Rooms, built as an Officers' Mess by G. T. Andrews in

1841–2 and little altered since. They were used for concerts, public meetings and entertainments, and nowadays are partly occupied by the city's main tourist and information centre. Next comes the **Theatre Royal**. There has been some sort of theatre in York since the early 18th century, when touring companies of actors visited the city. In 1734, a theatre was erected in the tennis court of Ingram House, near the Minster. This soon proved inadequate, and in 1744 the cloister of old St Leonard's Hospital was leased and the Theatre Royal was constructed on its undercroft. It had its heyday under the management of Tate Wilkinson (1766–1803), when it ranked among the best provincial theatres in the country and visiting actors included Sarah Siddons and J. P. Kemble. A period of decline followed which lasted until the 1930s, despite several refurbishings. The present delightful art nouveau interior, by F. A. Tugwell, dates from 1902. The façade (George Styan, 1879) is in a rather forbidding municipal gothic style, with Shakespeare and various of his characters appearing in the roundels. The foyer, in the form of a glass 'envelope' with concrete pillars, was designed by Patrick Gwynne and added in 1967. It is highly successful, one of the best examples of modern architecture in the city. The stage was modernised and the auditorium renovated at the same time.

Before crossing the other end of Duncombe Place, look to the left at the **Red House** (**46**), built in 1714 on the site of St Leonard's Hospital gateway for Sir William Robinson, a former Lord Mayor (the City Corporation tried to requisition it as the Lord Mayor's official residence, but failed). To the right of the front door can be seen the original

45 St Leonard's Place. The creation of a street 'for genteel private residences' on the site of the medieval St Leonard's Hospital was proposed in 1831, and in 1834 this terrace of nine houses was begun, to designs by John Harper; they were given a uniform frontage, but internal arrangements were left to each leaseholder. When the 99-year leases expired the properties reverted to the City Corporation, and are now Local Authority offices.

44 Nos. 49–51 Bootham, just beyond Bootham Bar – one of the most fashionable residential areas during the 18th century.

extinguishers for the torches that lit the owners home at night. Continue into Blake Street, to a place that the Red House's owners must often have frequented: the **Assembly Rooms** (1730–5), the fashionable meeting place of the gentry when York was the social capital of the north. (They are on the right of the street; to see the inside, which should not be missed, ask for the key at the Estate Office, 5 St Leonard's Place.) Designed by the famous Palladian architect Lord Burlington (a portrait of him, from Kneller's studio, hangs by the stairway in the City Art Gallery), the central hall (**47**), colonnaded with 52 Corinthian pillars, is quite unlike any other architecture in the city. It proved to be one of the most influential architectural designs of the early 18th century, but it was not to everyone's liking – Sarah Churchill, Duchess of Marlborough, complained that the pillars were so close together that it was impossible to pass between them (in the wide hooped skirt of conventional evening dress). The side openings were added later; originally the room was more severe in character. Towards the end of the century the York assemblies lost much of their popularity, as the gentry sought their pleasures further afield in London, and the Rooms fell into a state of neglect. After World War II they were rescued by the Corporation and reopened in 1951, when a glittering ball was held, attended by many of the descendants of the families who had financed the building with their subscriptions in the 18th century. The Rooms are still used nowadays for social functions, as well as for conferences and exhibitions. The grandeur of the colonnading is matched by the opulence of its colouring: the pillars are painted yellow with red-brown marbling, while the Corinthian capitals are picked out in green, purple and gold, and their colours are repeated in the entablature above. The façade was remodelled in 1828 by James Piggot Pritchett and Charles Watson (whose other work includes the Savings Bank in nearby St Helen's Square).

At the end of Blake Street cross St Helen's Square to the church of **St Helen**, which since the destruction of St Martin le Grand in the war has been the civic church, and is where the Lord Mayor and Corporation attend Harvest Thanksgiving in state every year. St Helen's was itself partly demolished in the 16th century, but was saved by the efforts of its parishioners, who obtained a private Act from Queen Mary to re-erect it. The west end and the tower (a copy of that of All Saints Pavement) were rebuilt in the 19th century, but otherwise the present structure is mainly 14th century. Although this was the parish church of the glass painters, many of whom lived and worked in nearby Stonegate during the Middle Ages – the coat of arms of the glass painters' guild can be seen in the west window of the south aisle – it has surprisingly little stained glass in comparison with other York churches. The best is the 15th-century glass in the west window (**48**), showing St Helen, the Virgin as Queen of Heaven, Edward the Confessor and St William of York. The late Norman font (**3**) is the best of its period in the city (the base is later).

Turn right outside the door and right again into **Stonegate**, which follows the course of the Roman Via Praetoria. Its name means 'stone paved street', and was first recorded in the early 12th century. This was the road along which all the stone for the building of the Minster was dragged. In the Middle Ages it was the scene of many colourful processions,

46 *Sir William Robinson, Lord Mayor in the early 18th century, had the Red House built for himself in 1714; the name may refer to the use, unusual in York, of brick, instead of stone, for an important building, and not to the colour of the brickwork of the main frontage. In 1724 Sir William resisted the city's attempts to acquire the house as the Mayor's official residence, and was thus instrumental in the building of the Mansion House (**26**), which was begun the following year. Dr John Burton the historian, the model for Dr Slop in Sterne's* Tristram Shandy, *lived in the Red House in the mid 18th century.*

and today it is probably York's most charming street. A pedestrian precinct, it is lined with substantial 15th- and 16th-century houses, many with late Georgian and Victorian shopfronts, and again the Minster closes the view, this time seen from the south (**49**). Nearly every building in the street has some pleasurable feature. On the left, notice the jolly frontage of Victorian Minton tiles designed to harmonise with the medieval structure (**9**). Mulberry Hall, opposite, is an especially notable example of an early-15th-century house; until the Reformation it was the residence of the Bishop of Chester. The late-17th-century Old Punch Bowl on the right is one of the oldest inns in the city, originally a coffee house frequented by those of the Whig political persuasion. One cannot miss the other pub in Stonegate, for a large sign, first erected in 1753, straddles the street proclaiming the presence along a narrow alley of Ye Olde Starre (early 17th century). To the left a narrow passage leads to the remains of the oldest dwelling in the city, the Norman House of *c*1180 (**4**). This was a two-storey building, probably with a wooden undercroft. The main room or hall would have been on the upper floor, where the inside of a two-light window with waterleaf capitals can be seen. Back in Stonegate, above the entrance to Coffee Yard crouches the figure of a judicial-looking red devil, a symbol of the printer's 'devils', the boys who fetched type for their masters. York's first newspaper, the *York Mercury*, was printed here in 1719. Coffee Yard has been so called since the 17th century, when the first coffee houses were opened in York, and its buildings date mainly from that time. As you cross High Petergate into Minster Gates, look up at the corner of the shop on the left to see John

47 *The Assembly Rooms, designed by Lord Burlington in 1730, when York was at the height of its importance as the social centre of the north. The proportions (112×40×40ft) and the colonnading were taken from the model of an Egyptian hall by the Roman architect Vitruvius, as reported by Burlington's great inspiration, Palladio – the directors of the enterprise having told him 'We entirely leave to your lordship to do in what manner you shall think proper.'*

Wolstenholme's carving of Minerva, goddess of wisdom and charity (**50**). She is resting (with her owl) on a pile of books, for this was formerly known as Bookbinders' Alley on account of the area's strong associations with the bookselling and printing trades. These continue in the present day, and in general York is an excellent city for lovers of second-hand books. The Minster Gates used to stand here, marking the entrance to the Minster Liberty, through which one could proceed only on foot.

Turn right into Deangate to look at the Roman column, 30 ft (9 m) tall, found during the excavation of the Minster south transept in 1969 and believed to have stood in the main hall of the Roman fortress. It was re-erected here in 1971 (some think upside-down) to mark the 1900th anniversary of the founding of the city. Take a short cut through the Minster ground (on the right is the Minster Song School, 1832), past the spectacular east end of the cathedral, to **St William's College** (**52**), recognisable by its long half-timbered upper storey oversailing the ashlar ground floor. It was formed in 1465–7 as a home for the Minster chantry priests by extending what had been the residence of the Prior of Hexham. After the Reformation it passed into private hands, and when Charles I moved his court to York in 1642 it was used to house the royal printing press. Subsequently it served a variety of purposes and became increasingly dilapidated until the beginning of this century, when it was restored by the architect Temple Moore. Several of its features are due to him, including the oriel windows in the façade, derived from a single original survivor in the delightful inner courtyard. Above the outer doorway is the seated figure of St William, and under the eaves at the ends of the beams are carved figures of the Virgin and Child and of St Christopher. The charming row of shopfronts, a Regency addition, was wisely retained at the time of the restoration.

Continue towards Minster Yard, with the chapter house now in full view, pausing to look down the attractive cobbled Chapter House Street to the right. This roughly follows the line of the Roman Via Decumana, which led from the back of the headquarters building to the north-eastern gate of the fortress. On the right in Minster Yard is the **Treasurer's House** (**51**), so called because it is on the site of the medieval residence of the Treasurer to the Minster, a powerful functionary in the Church of the Middle Ages. The office became extinct at the time of the Reformation – as the then incumbent tersely put it, 'being plundered of all its treasure, it [the Minster] had no need of a treasurer' (but the post was revived in 1936). The house passed to Archbishop Young and was largely rebuilt in the early 17th century, especially in the 1630s and 1640s, when it was owned by the Archbishop's great-grandson Thomas Young, though certain elements are later, such as the ogee gables (c1700). The present appearance of the interior is due to the restoration effected at the beginning of this century by the owner, the Yorkshire industrialist Frank Green, and his adviser, Temple Moore, which has made it one of the most attractive houses in the city. The hall was completely remodelled, and now rises through two floors. The staircase, which leads to a half-timbered gallery, was based on one at Knole in Kent. The drawing room has been described as 'perhaps the most beautiful room in York', while the dining room, refitted in the 18th century, has moulded plaster panels

52 *St William's College, built on a courtyard plan like the colleges of Oxford and Cambridge, was originally (1465) the home of the Minster's chantry priests. After the Reformation it changed hands several times, and by the 18th century it was being used as tenements, gradually decaying; restored by Temple Moore in 1906, it now serves Diocesan purposes once more.*

51 *The south-west entrance of the 17th-century Treasurer's House, on the site of the medieval residence of the Treasurer to the Minster.*

and a richly decorated stucco ceiling. The whole house is filled with valuable furniture and is kept in excellent condition by the National Trust, to whom Mr Green presented it in 1930. The charming semi-formal garden has terraces, statues and an abundance of flowers. Adjoining the Treasurer's House is Gray's Court, and behind its back façade can be seen 12th- and early-13th-century remains of the original house of the Treasurer. Also restored by Temple Moore, Gray's Court is now occupied by the History Department of the College of Ripon and York St John.

A gentle stroll past the well-cared-for Georgian and neo-Georgian houses of Minster Yard leads to Dean's Park and the **Minster Library**, housed in what used to be the chapel (13th century) of the Archbishop's Palace; it is open to the public, and some of the Minster's vast collection of books and manuscripts can be viewed. The late-12th-century arcade (**5**) is the only other remnant of the palace that once stood here. Its destruction is said to have been started by Archbishop Young (1561–8), when he removed and sold lead from the roof of the great hall to buy an estate for his son. The ruins and the surrounding land were granted to Sir Richard Ingram *c*1616 and he built a house here, laying out the grounds as pleasure gardens; the house was demolished in 1814. Nowadays the Archbishop resides at Bishopthorpe Palace, about 2 miles from the city centre (**6**). Our walk concludes as we leave Dean's Park through the Walker iron gates (1839) outside the west front of the Minster.

Places of Interest around York

Beningbrough Hall (C3)

Built for John Bourchier in 1716, and so good an example of a late baroque English country house that it used to be attributed to Vanbrugh; it is now thought to be by William Thornton (died 1721), who worked with Hawksmoor at Beverley, and whose skill as a joiner can be admired in the expert woodcarving of the main rooms and staircase. Nearly 100 pictures from the National Portrait Gallery are on display, including paintings by Reynolds, Gainsborough and Kneller, well set off by the excellent 18th-century furniture.

Beverley (F4,**53**)

From early medieval times pilgrims flocked to the shrine of St John of Beverley (Bishop of York 705–18), in the Minster which he had founded. Henry V came here to give thanks after his victory at Agincourt. In the late 14th century the flourishing local wool trade made Beverley the tenth wealthiest town of England (in terms of taxes paid), and several of its buildings testify to its medieval prosperity. The North Bar, one of the four gateways that marked the town's entrances in the 15th century, stands on the most impressive approach to the centre. The Minster, with its beautiful and imposing exterior characterised by soaring twin towers, is a landmark for miles around. One of the finest gothic churches in England, it was largely rebuilt in its present form in the early 13th century. In the 18th century Hawksmoor advised on its restoration. The fine fittings of the interior include the marvellous 14th-century Percy Tomb in the north choir aisle, an elaborately decorated gabled stone canopy, delicately carved with foliage and figures; choir stalls of 1520 with 68 varied misericords of people and animals; and the late-12th-century black marble font with a sumptuously carved cover of 1713. St Mary's, begun in the 12th century and completed in 1520 with the rebuilding of the central tower (crowned with 16 pinnacles), was the town merchants' church in the Middle Ages. The hauntingly lovely interior has a sequence of richly carved, moulded and painted roofs: the 40 panels of the chancel roof bear paintings (1445) of kings from Brutus to Henry VI. The choir stalls are early 15th century, and have splendid misericords. Other buildings to note while wandering around this charming town include the Guildhall and Courthouse in Register Square, with a Doric

53 *The nave of Beverley Minster, looking west. Built of creamy white limestone in the 14th century, it is modelled on the design of the 13th-century choir – an interesting instance of medieval architects opting for consistency of effect at the cost of building in an old-fashioned style. The huge west window was completed c1450.*

façade (1832) fronting a building of 1760 designed by William Middleton. The stucco ceiling of the courtroom, with the figure of Justice enthroned in the middle, is particularly well worth seeing. In Saturday Market the central feature is the Market Cross (1714), and here and in the smaller Wednesday Market are several substantial Georgian houses. Ancient common lands known as Beverley Pastures surround the town with green spaces on three sides.

Byland Abbey (C1)

Ruins of a very large Cistercian foundation, 12th and 13th century, in the embrace of the wooded slopes of the Byland valley. The remaining cliffs of stone against the sky, especially the towering south-eastern survival, are reminiscent of a Cotman watercolour. Interesting floor-tile colours and patterns, particularly in what was the south transept.

Castle Howard (D2, 54)

One of England's greatest houses, a palace of robust magnificence set in the empty landscape of North Yorkshire. Howards have lived on the site since 1571. When their castle burnt down in 1693, Charles Howard, 3rd Earl of Carlisle, commissioned the 35-year-old Sir John Vanbrugh to build a new mansion. The choice remains unexplained – Vanbrugh, a captain in the Marines and a successful playwright, had never designed a building in his life. Yet he turned out to be an architect of genius (later he designed Blenheim Palace for the Duke of Marlborough). Hawksmoor, Wren's most brilliant pupil, was employed as consultant. By 1709 the main part of the house was finished.

The two chief façades are in strong contrast: the one facing the garden has a gaiety absent from the forbiddingly impressive entrance front. The domed entrance hall is spectacular. The memorable tunnel-like vaulted corridors are probably by Hawksmoor. The Long Gallery contains excellent pictures (e.g. two Holbein portraits, of Henry VIII and of Thomas Howard, Duke of Norfolk). The earl spent even more on the grounds than on the house. The park extends over 1000 acres and is famous for its series of ornamental buildings, which includes an obelisk and a pyramid. A pleasant walk from the house along a grass terrace leads to Vanbrugh's Temple of the Winds (1724–6), the perfection of 18th-century architectural charm. Energetic visitors should proceed to the Howard mausoleum, designed by Hawksmoor. Twenty immense columns supporting a shallow dome stand isolated on the brow of a slight hill amongst fields and trees. This is a monumental work of great emotional power.

Coxwold (B1)

Neat village of mellow stone houses (several of them 17th century), its main street rising to the 15th-century church. Opposite and a little further on is Shandy Hall, the modest home (1760–8), now sympathetically restored and lovingly maintained, of Laurence Sterne, novelist and vicar

54 *A dramatic view of the south or garden front of Castle Howard, under a lowering Yorkshire sky. The façade is not quite symmetrical: the pavilion at the left-hand end was built after Vanbrugh's death, and not to his design. It is part of the west wing, added by Sir Thomas Robinson during 1753–9, which incorporates a shallow dome (just visible behind the pavilion).*

of Coxwold (see above, p. 22). The whole house and garden are redolent of 18th-century cultivated middle-class domestic life; especially evocative is the tiny study where Sterne worked on *Tristram Shandy* and *A Sentimental Journey*, lined with contemporary editions of the books he would have had in his library.

Fountains Abbey and Studley Royal Country Park (A2, 55)

Fountains, a vast ruin in a glorious setting, is the best-preserved abbey in England. In 1132 a group of Benedictine monks left St Mary's Abbey in York because they found its relaxed way of life distasteful. They went to Skelldale – wild and uninhabited but with the advantage of natural springs in the rocky hillsides, from which the new abbey took its name. The monks adopted the Cistercian rule. A great part of their first abbey was destroyed in 1147 in reprisal for their connivance at the deposition of the Archbishop of York; rebuilding started at once and continued into the 1170s. The transepts and nave of the church survive remarkably complete, their pointed arches resting on massive piers of Romanesque form. The east end was rebuilt in the early 13th century and given an eastern transept. The only major subsequent development was the huge tower added to the end of the north transept in the early 16th century and now the most eye-catching element of the ruins. It was a proud gesture, but only a few years later the abbey was dissolved, yielding a large fortune in lands and furnishings to Henry VIII. The monastic buildings are arranged around a cloister. Their most impressive feature is the west range, 300 ft (91.5 m) long, which housed the lay brothers' refectory above a long vaulted cellar that still survives.

The site passed to Sir Stephen Proctor, who in 1611 built himself a large house, Fountains Hall, using stones from the ruins. In 1768 the Fountains estate was acquired by the owner of the adjoining Studley Royal lands, William Aislabie. His father, John, had been Chancellor of the Exchequer at the time of the South Sea Bubble scandal. Expelled from Parliament, John Aislabie retired to his estates and laid out the ornamental gardens that can still be seen, complete with lake, canal, pools, temples and gothick tower. William extended the landscaping to include the abbey ruins – surely the most magnificent garden building in the world. The Aislabies' own house has been demolished, but not the parish church, built 1871–8 for the Marchioness of Ripon, whose family inherited the Aislabie lands. It too is part of the landscape, standing at the end of a lime tree avenue that focuses on the distant west front of Ripon Cathedral. The architect was William Burges, famous for Cardiff Castle and Cork Cathedral – one of the most original Victorian architects. No expense was spared. The exterior is lavishly ornamented, and the chancel is dazzlingly rich: black, red and green marble, sculpture, alabaster, gilding, a mosaic floor, stained glass windows with double tracery – all of superb craftsmanship – combine in an ensemble which unites religious fervour with aesthetic intensity.

55 *The magnificent ruins of Fountains Abbey evoke the splendour of medieval monastic architecture more completely than anything else in England. The church's great tower, 170ft high, is a 16th-century addition to the 12th- and 13th-century building. The living quarters were built over the River Skell, visible in the foreground; it was customary for monasteries to be built near running water, which provided drainage.*

Harewood House (A4, 56)

Harewood is an estate village: classical terraces line the main street leading to the park gates and form part of a long avenue. The medieval church in the grounds is all that remains of the original village, swept away when the Lascelles family landscaped the park. The house, begun in 1759 to designs by the York architect John Carr, was built of stone quarried on the estate. The exterior is weighty, even a little ponderous – unlike the elegantly sumptuous interiors, which are by Robert Adam. His refined use of painted plasterwork is perfectly complemented by the contemporary furniture, designed for the house by Chippendale. These wonderful ensembles are the setting for a superb collection of pictures, not only family portraits but also paintings by Giovanni Bellini, Titian, Veronese and El Greco. The south façade was remodelled in 1843 by Sir Charles Barry, who also refitted some of the rooms and laid out a parterre. Its stately formality makes a piquant contrast with the airy expanses of the parkland, designed by Capability Brown. There are also Pleasure Grounds to be enjoyed: a walk through woodland stocked with exotic trees leads to a lake surrounded by rhododendrons (vivid in early summer). Rare species of birds are bred in the Bird Garden, where a tropical house accommodates birds from hot climates.

Harrogate (A3)

A spa town that boomed in the 19th century, when the waters (it has both sulphurous and chalybeate springs) were consumed at the rate of 1000

glasses a morning. The Royal Pump Room (1842) now houses a museum, but still provides refreshments and concerts under the glas dome of the Sun Pavilion.

In the Royal Baths (1887) fin de siècle meets art nouveau, damped down by the northern climate but colourfully decorated with enamelled tiles. The wide open green spaces (former commons), the public parks, and the solid hotels and their gardens make modern Harrogate a relaxing shopping and conference centre.

Helmsley (C1)

Picturesque and unspoilt town, rich in old inns and with a stream running through the middle of it. The castle dominates the town and its approaches and is even more impressive as you walk up to it, the four-storey keep with turrets and battlements towering above. Pleasing views from the bailey, of Duncombe Place to the west and the tiled and slated roofs of Helmsley to the east. Remaining buildings date from 1200 to 1587, the most recent being the range north of the tower, which still has some panelling and plasterwork.

Kirkham Priory (D2, 57)

Founded *c*1125 for the Augustinian order by Judge Walter l'Espec as a memorial to his son, who had died in a hunting accident in the woods nearby; it is now mainly romantically overgrown ruins. The splendid late-13th-century gatehouse is carved with friezes, heraldic shields and sculptures – of St George and the dragon (left), David and Goliath (right) and, above, Christ in an almond-shaped glory picked out with ballflower decoration, St Bartholomew and St Philip. Several of the canons' domestic arrangements can still be made out, e.g. the drainage channels in the reredorter and the layout of the lavatorium, which has fine blank arcading on its back wall. An elaborate Norman doorway with very varied carving survives from the original church.

Knaresborough (A3)

Perched in a strong defensive position above the River Nid, the castle, which in 1170 harboured Thomas à Beckett's assassins after his murder, now consists chiefly of a keep on three floors (*c*1310–40) and an impressive dungeon, radially vaulted from a central pillar. The architecture above is not easy to understand, and may show signs of hurried alteration in a military emergency; during the Civil War, General Fairfax besieged the castle and starved it into surrender. The river is dramatically traversed by the railway, on a castellated bridge. Below is Mother Shipton's Cave, a small, dark, mercifully dry grotto. It is associated with a noted 16th-century witch (but the prophecies attributed to her were a 19th-century invention). Nearby, in the Dropping Well, can be seen the action of its high calcium content, which rapidly 'petrifies' anything left in it. The market square is the focus of the attractive, mainly 18th-century town; the chemist's shop here opened in 1720 and claims to be the oldest established in England.

Newby Hall, Skelton (A2)

The house was begun in 1705 for the coal-mining magnate Sir Edward Blackett. In 1748 it was sold to the Weddell family, whose descendants still live here. Robert Adam carried out major alterations for William Weddell, a wealthy art-lover, c1767–80. Most of the principal rooms were redecorated by him, and a very beautiful gallery was added to house Weddell's collection of antique sculpture. Adam's interiors are the last word in refined richness – delicately stuccoed and sensitively painted. Recent restoration by the present owners is both scholarly and inspired, and they are giving the same attention to the gardens and grounds. Near the entrance gates is Skelton's parish church of Christ the Consoler, built 1871–2 in memory of Frederick Vyner, the heir to Newby, murdered by brigands in Greece. The architect was William Burges, who designed the contemporary and even more lavish church at Studley Royal (see Fountains) for Frederick's sister, the Marchioness of Ripon. Skelton is the more picturesque composition, as befits its less formal position; its rich decoration includes much vigorous sculpture and good stained glass. Wild strawberries in the churchyard.

57 Kirkham Priory, now in ruins, was founded for an order of Augustinian canons in the early 12th century; this gatehouse dates from the late 13th century, and is elaborately decorated with carving and sculpture. On the second stage are figures of St George and the dragon (left) and David and Goliath (right); above is a figure of Christ, flanked by St Bartholemew and St Philip.

Pickering (D1)

Near the moors, and with an upland feel. The church dominates from a distance, and is approached by footpaths and flights of steps. Its (restored) series of mid-15th-century wall paintings, one of the most complete in England, gives a good idea of the liveliness of medieval church interiors. In rather strip-cartoon style they present doctrine (the Passion and Resurrection), narrative (life of St Catherine), edification (Acts of Mercy) and warnings (enormous hell mouth for the Descent into Hell). The castle dates from between the late 12th and early 14th centuries, and most English kings of that time hunted from it in Pickering Forest. It has an imposing curtain wall with square projecting towers, the ground falling away sharply to the west; the keep itself is set on a high motte, and the inner bailey also contains remains of two halls and a (restored) 13th-century chapel. From Pickering the North Yorkshire Moors Railway (part steam) runs to Grosmont through 18 miles of the beautiful scenery of the North York Moors National Park.

Pontefract (B5)

The castle (58), in which Richard II was imprisoned and murdered, changed hands three times during the Civil War and was eventually rased by the Parliamentarians; its ruins now form a recreation ground. The oldest visible parts are 12th century – sections of the wall, one of the gates, and foundations and the chancel arch of the apsed chapel. The wall of the keep, which had the shape of a clover leaf, is 13th century, standing on an 11th-century mound. Micklegate, Horsefair and Bridge St make a pleasant walk away from the castle. In the Market Place note the attractive Town Hall, 1785, and go on to the far end to see the Butter Cross, 1734.

Rievaulx Abbey (C1, 59)

One of England's most spectacular ruins, in the romantically beautiful valley of Ryedale. It was a Cistercian abbey, founded by a mission sent by one of the order's founders, St Bernard of Clairvaux, in 1131. The ruins fill a narrow site between hillside and the Rye, and are dominated by the remains of the great church. The nave has largely disappeared, but the transepts and the lavish chancel still tower up to their full three tiers. The rebuilding of the chancel in the mid 13th century left the abbey in debt and it seems never to have recovered: at its dissolution it housed only 22 monks, using buildings designed for several hundred. The ruins of the monastic quarters are very extensive, the remains of the huge refectory, built on a high undercroft, being the most memorable.

Rievaulx Terrace (C1)

Laid out in the 1750s by Thomas Duncombe III, whose family had acquired the lands and abbey of Rievaulx in the 17th century and built Duncombe Park there. The wide curving grass terrace with Grecian temples at either end – one Doric, the other Ionic – is bordered by trees

58 *The keep of Pontefract Castle, formerly one of Yorkshire's most impressive strongholds, destroyed during the Civil War.*

59 *Rievaulx Abbey ruins: a view through the 13th-century north arcade of the choir, towards the south transept (on the right). Part of the monastic buildings, including the chapter house, can be seen beyond on the left. The raised area in the choir is the site of the high altar.*

and shrubs on one side and on the other falls away dramatically to give, through clearings at calculated intervals, a variety of exhilarating views of the abbey ruins in the valley below.

Ripon (A2)

A small, compact town, with narrow winding streets that all seem to lead to the spacious Market Square or to the stately west front of the cathedral. St Wilfrid, Bishop of York, rebuilt the church here *c*670, and the crypt of his building still exists; it is among the earliest Christian remains in England. Now used as the cathedral treasury, it originally housed a relic chamber (the narrow stairs and passages provided access for pilgrims), and has the feel of a primitive stronghold. The present cathedral was begun *c*1180 and completed with the building of the west front, *c*1220–30. This is massive and starkly simple – rows of lancet windows with little embellishment. By contrast, the chancel, which was reconstructed *c*1300, is richly decorated: the clerestory has double tracery, the sedilia are lushly carved, there are delightful misericords in the 15th-century choir stalls, and the wooden ceiling contains excellent 14th-century bosses. In the 15th century fears for the safety of the crossing tower caused drastic alterations, which resulted in the present ungainly appearance of the crossing itself. One pier and the north and west arches of the original building were retained, while the rest was rebuilt. Look out for the monument to William Weddell, underneath a little cupola set into the south transept wall – a bust by Nollekens, another version of which presides over Weddell's sculpture galleries at Newby Hall (q.v.).

Selby (C4)

A small market town with a few imposing Georgian houses, an 18th-century wooden bridge over the River Ouse, and a splendid abbey church (**60, 61**) that survived the Reformation. The different stages of the church's construction are marked by clearly visible shifts of style. The oldest existing parts are the Norman transepts and the magnificent nave, which changes from monumental Romanesque at its east end to rich gothic in the gallery. The chancel was rebuilt *c*1280–1340; its glory is the huge east window, in which sumptuously flowing tracery combine with much of the original 14th-century glass to magical effect. Notice also the lofty, richly carved 15th-century font cover, and some strange medieval stone figures peering down into the chancel from the parapet in front of the clerestory windows.

60 *In the nave of Selby Abbey, looking east. The choir screen and the pulpit, like most of the abbey's woodwork, were erected c1909 during restoration after the fire which gutted this great medieval church in 1906. The flag of the United States hanging in the choir is close to a 14th-century window that includes the earliest known representation of the Washington family's coat of arms, from which the Stars and Stripes were derived.*

Skelton (C3)

This trim village has a famous church, a treat for lovers of medieval architecture. It is all of a piece, and was built *c*1240 by masons who worked on York Minster (as their marks on the stonework prove). The style is close to the Minster's transepts. The church is lavishly decorated with carving around its lancet windows and splendid south doorway, but, oddly, is extremely small – only 55 ft (17 m) long. The imposing piers of

the two-bay arcades and the chancel arch totally overpower the interior. Perhaps a much larger building was planned; but evidence is lacking. The church has been well restored, initially by the 19-year-old Henry Graham (son of the rector of St Saviour's, York, he died shortly after finishing the work in 1818). The very attractive churchyard is carefully tended to encourage a wide variety of wildlife (in summer, willow warblers and spotted fly-catchers nest here).

Temple Newsam House (A4)

The original house was built in the early 16th century by Thomas, Lord Darcy, who was executed by Henry VIII. It passed to the Ingram family, London merchants who later developed many connections with York, and in the 1630s it was altered and extended, acquiring its present Jacobean appearance (little modified by rebuilding of the south wing in 1796). Leeds Corporation bought it in 1922, and it is now a very good museum and art gallery, housing an outstanding collection and full of period furniture. The Chinese Room has hand-painted Chinese wallpaper and Chippendale Chinese furniture.

61 *The lavishly carved Norman west doorway of Selby Abbey, the lay people's entrance to their part of the otherwise monastic church.*

PLACES
OF INTEREST
AROUND
YORK

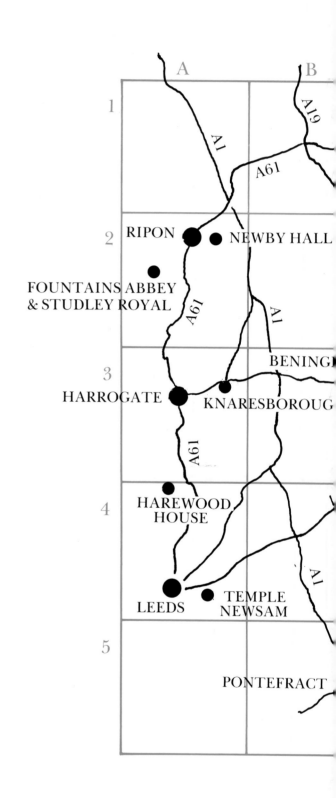

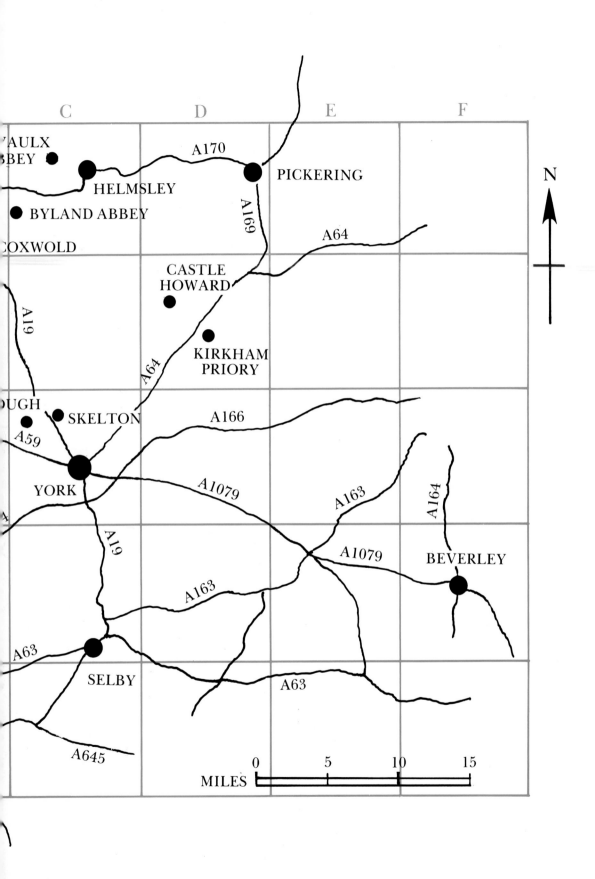